Horrible Histories
DEAD!

CONTENTS

Watts Books
London • New York • Sydney

DYING

All living things die. It's the one thing we can all be certain of. In the past, dying was a lot more unpleasant than it is today. The average age of people when they died in the Stone Age was less than eighteen years. The main causes of death were disease and violence.

Fortunately, in western countries nowadays, most people die peacefully in old age. There are even special nursing homes called hospices to care for people who are dying of incurable illnesses.

On the island of Samoa sick old chiefs used to ask to be buried alive.

The image of the Grim Reaper is often associated with death.

The lifespan of the elephant is roughly the same as that of humans - about seventy years.

Some species of mayfly live for only a few hours after they emerge from their larvae.

Different cultures have different ways of dying. Old people of the Omaha tribe of Native Americans would stay behind when the rest of their family group moved camp. They were left enough food for just a few days.

Some species of birds live to a great age. Cocky, a male sulphur-crested cockatoo, died in London in 1982 aged over 80.

The most famous hospice in the world was founded by a nun called Mother Teresa. Her hospice was founded to look after people dying on the streets of Calcutta.

Er... I can't think of anything! Err...

Buddhists believe that their dying thoughts will have an important influence on their next life.

Some Hindus try to say the word 'om' with their last breath. They believe that this may help them to escape the cycle of reincarnation.

Trees live a lot longer than animals. The oldest tree is thought to be 'General Sherman', a giant sequoia tree in California about 3,000 years old.

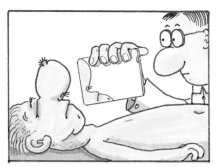

Test for death: Mirror
Breath should cause steam to appear
on a mirror held to the mouth.

Test for death: Pulse
A pulse shows that the
heart is still beating.

Test for death: Light
A modern test for brain stem death is to see
if the pupils of the eye contract in bright light.

TESTING FOR DEATH

Brain
stem

Death doesn't happen to all parts of a body at once. It takes time. For instance, brain cells die four minutes after the heart has stopped beating, but arterial grafts can be made seventy-two hours later. So it's not always easy to know exactly when somebody is dead.

The effects of extreme cold, called hypothermia, and of certain trance-like states such as catalepsy, have often been mistaken for death because breathing and heartbeat couldn't be detected. In fact, in the past, burial alive by mistake may have been quite common.

Nowadays, death is said to have happened when the brain stem stops working. The brain stem sits at the back of the skull. It controls vital body functions such as heartbeat and breathing. Modern instruments can detect breathing and heartbeat very accurately.

Queen Anne Boleyn's head
continued to move its lips
after it had been chopped off.

Around 1308 the philosopher Duns Scotus was buried in a vault in Cologne. When the vault was reopened shortly after, Duns Scotus was found outside his coffin. His hands were torn from trying to open the door of the vault. He had been buried alive.

Test for death: Blood
The Romans would chop off a finger to see if it bled.

Test for Death: Smoke
Some tribes of Native Americans would blow smoke
up the bottom to test for any revival of life.

Test for Death: Nipple Forceps
In the nineteenth century Dr Josat invented
a pair of nipple forceps to test for reaction to
pain. Reaction to pain is also a modern test
for brain stem death.

Many people stay up all night beside
the body of a dead friend or relative.
One reason for this custom is to make
sure that the dead person is really
dead and not just unconscious.

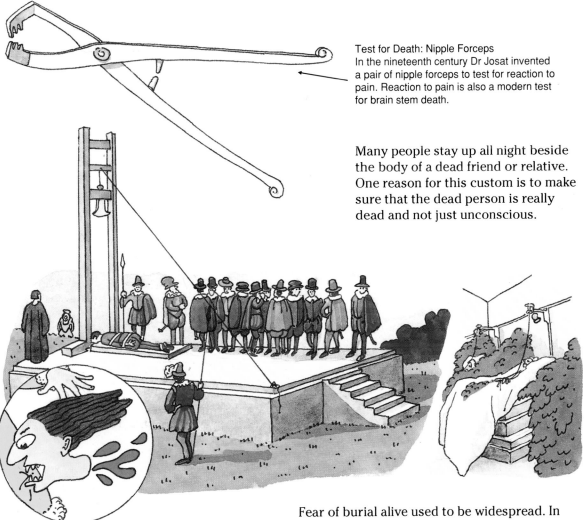

In 1541 the head of a woman guillotined
on the Halifax gibbet flew through the
air and gripped the clothing of a
passerby with its teeth.

Fear of burial alive used to be widespread. In
the Munich Waiting Mortuary, founded in 1791,
corpses were kept for up to seventy-two hours
in a sloping position before burial. Cords were
attached to their fingers in such a way that the
slightest movement would cause bells to ring.

DEAD BODIES

After death the muscles of the body relax. Relaxation starts in the jaw which falls open, and then spreads out through the body. At the same time, because the blood has stopped circulating, it sinks and causes stains on the skin which look like bruises. About six hours later, rigor mortis sets in. This is a stiffening of the muscles which again starts at the jaw and spreads out through the body. Rigor mortis normally lasts about thirty hours, then relaxation of the muscles spreads out once more from the jaw. Rigor mortis may set in immediately if death occurs at a time of stress. This is why suicides may be found gripping the revolver or sword with which they killed themselves.

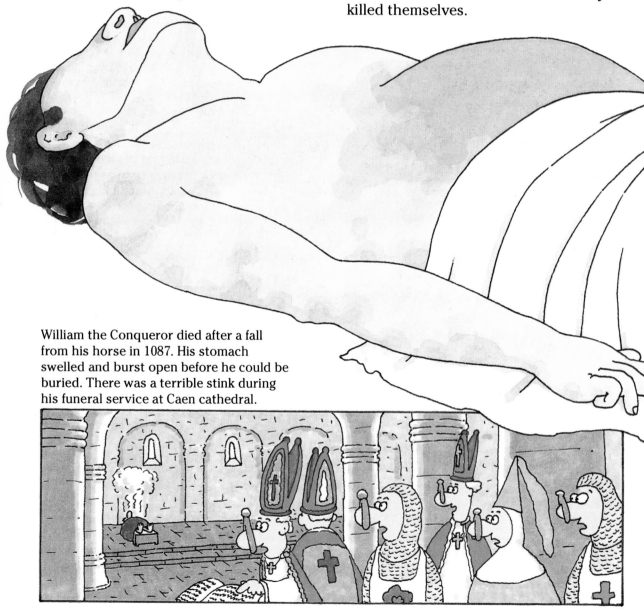

William the Conqueror died after a fall from his horse in 1087. His stomach swelled and burst open before he could be buried. There was a terrible stink during his funeral service at Caen cathedral.

In a warm climate, putrefaction, or rotting, starts after a few days. First, a greenish tinge appears around the stomach and spreads outwards. Then, the stomach swells up with gases like a balloon, and can burst open. Finally, liquefaction (going runny) starts at the eyeballs and finishes with the stomach, liver and womb (in women). Bones do not putrefy.

In subzero temperatures, bodies do not decompose (rot).

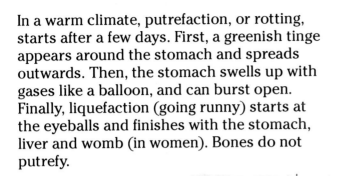

A 45 year old woman died standing upright in a timber yard in the town of Wahncau in Germany. Rigor mortis had set in at the moment of death.

eek!

If death occurs during exercise, rigor mortis can set in immediately. During the charge of the Light Brigade in 1854, an officer's head was blown from his body. The body galloped on upright and stiff in the saddle with his sword still held high.

FUNERALS

About two million people die every year in the USA alone, so dealing with dead bodies is a major industry. Normally the first people to handle the dead are nurses and doctors. They tidy the hair and nails, tie up the jaw, put a plug in the bottom and probably they will remove dentures and jewellery. From that point the funeral directors, or undertakers, take over. They take the body away in a temporary coffin and prepare it for burial or cremation. The funeral director's job includes embalming the corpse, supplying the coffin, sending out invitations for the funeral and booking time at a crematorium or buying a plot of land for a burial. In the past, undertakers were often carpenters, because carpenters knew how to make coffins.

The coffin should be the height of the body plus two inches, and it should be the width of the shoulders across. Traditionally, coffins were made of oak or elm; nowadays, they are more likely to be made of veneered chipboard.

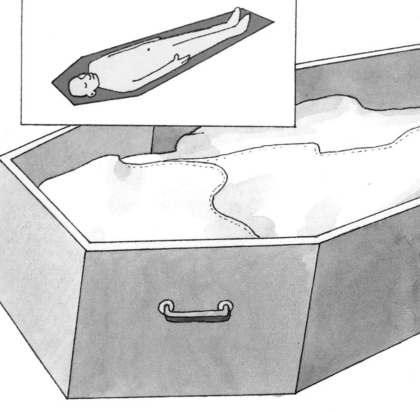

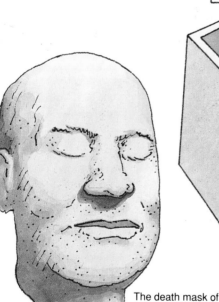

The death mask of Samuel Johnson

Death masks often are made by moulding clay around the face of a dead person. When the clay is removed there is a perfect impression of the dead person's face on the inside of it, and it can be used as a mould.

Coffin linings are made of base and side sheets which are attached to the coffin, a loose flap to cover the body and a face cloth to cover the head.

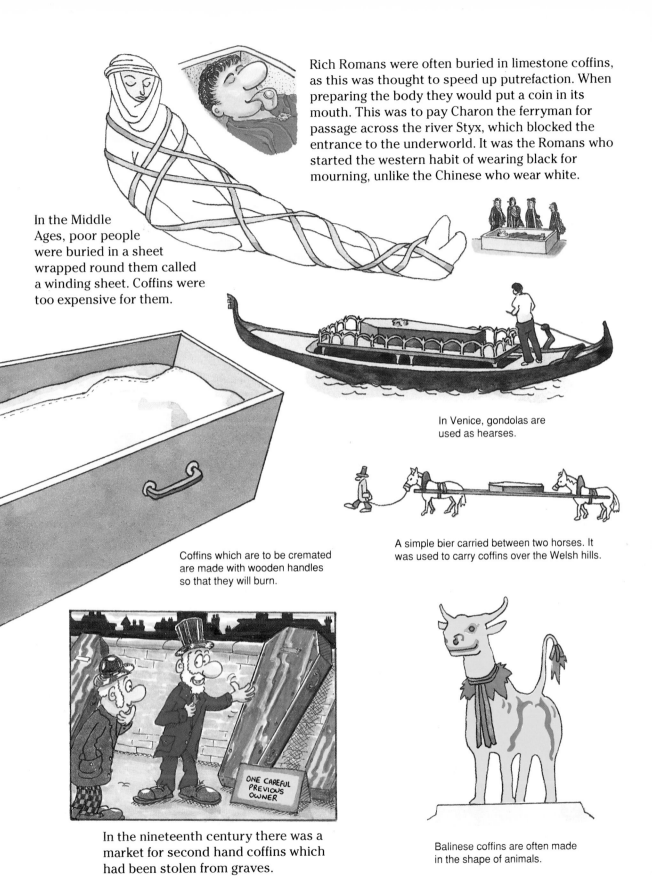

Rich Romans were often buried in limestone coffins, as this was thought to speed up putrefaction. When preparing the body they would put a coin in its mouth. This was to pay Charon the ferryman for passage across the river Styx, which blocked the entrance to the underworld. It was the Romans who started the western habit of wearing black for mourning, unlike the Chinese who wear white.

In the Middle Ages, poor people were buried in a sheet wrapped round them called a winding sheet. Coffins were too expensive for them.

In Venice, gondolas are used as hearses.

A simple bier carried between two horses. It was used to carry coffins over the Welsh hills.

Coffins which are to be cremated are made with wooden handles so that they will burn.

In the nineteenth century there was a market for second hand coffins which had been stolen from graves.

Balinese coffins are often made in the shape of animals.

9

Home guide to head shrinking

Remove the head from the body.

Make a cut from the back of the neck to the crown of the head.

Remove the skin from the skull and discard the skull.

Sew the eyelids together. Sew the lips together.

EMBALMING

Nowadays many bodies are embalmed. It makes them look peaceful and it stops them smelling before the funeral.

The body is first placed on a trolley and washed in soap and water. Then embalming fluid is pumped into it through an opening in a vein, normally near the armpit. Embalming fluid is a mixture of preservative (usually formaldehyde), disinfectant and colouring. As the fluid spreads through the veins, the body regains a healthy pink colour. Then, after four to six pints have been pumped in, the blood is drained out of the body through another opened vein into a vacuum container on the floor.

The process of replacing the blood with embalming fluid takes about three-quarters of an hour. Afterwards, a surgical instrument called a trocar is plunged into the abdomen and scooped around until all the soft tissue has been removed. Cavity fluid is then pumped in to fill up the empty space.

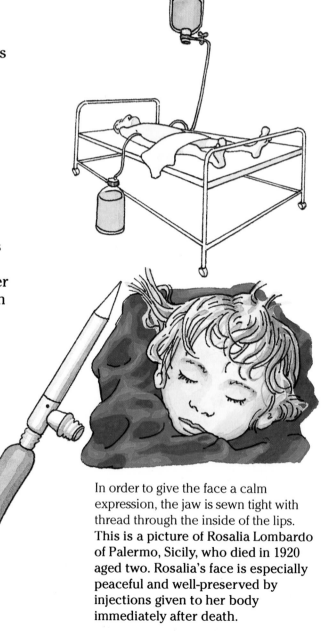

In order to give the face a calm expression, the jaw is sewn tight with thread through the inside of the lips. This is a picture of Rosalia Lombardo of Palermo, Sicily, who died in 1920 aged two. Rosalia's face is especially peaceful and well-preserved by injections given to her body immediately after death.

10

Boil the scalp and face for two hours.

Place hot stones in the scalp to shrink the skin.

Smoke overnight.

Hang above the fireplace.

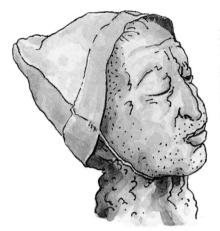

Bodies are sometimes embalmed naturally. Tollund Man, who was probably a fertility sacrifice to the goddess Ertha around 500 BC, was preserved intact in a peat bog until discovered in 1950 at Tollund in Denmark. His features are so well-preserved that even the stubble of his beard is completely visible.

Tourists queue to see Lenin's body in his open tomb outside the walls of the Kremlin, Moscow.

A preserved head from ancient Peru. A cactus spine has been inserted through the lips.

Perhaps the most famous body to be embalmed this century is that of Lenin, the leader of the Russian revolution. The body is kept in a temperature-controlled mausoleum in Red Square, Moscow, and is visited by thousands of tourists every year. Every eighteen months the body is taken out and soaked in a special preservative fluid.

In ancient Babylon, bodies were sometimes embalmed in honey. It is said that the body of Alexander the Great was preserved like this.

The Egyptians had several different beliefs about the after-life. Here is one of them:

Ba, the soul, could enter or leave the body at will. It was pictured as a human-headed bird.

After death, Ba made a dangerous journey to the Kingdom of Osiris. A ferryman with eyes in the back of his head took Ba across a river.

Osiris judged new souls at midnight. Ba was then weighed against the feather of virtue. If he had been good, the feather would be heavier.

MUMMIES AND EMBALMING

The ancient Egyptians believed that it was necessary to preserve the body of a dead person in order for that dead person to be reborn. Belief in resurrection after death was centred around the cult of the god Osiris. Osiris was born a man, died, and was mummified by the heavenly doctor Anubis; he was then reborn as a god. The Egyptians believed that by following the same process of mummification, they too could be resurrected. Millions of Egyptians were mummified during the course of the ancient Egyptian civilisation.

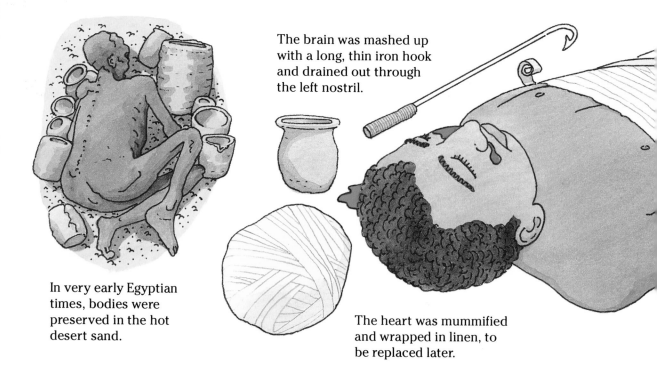

The brain was mashed up with a long, thin iron hook and drained out through the left nostril.

In very early Egyptian times, bodies were preserved in the hot desert sand.

The heart was mummified and wrapped in linen, to be replaced later.

Good souls were given land in the kingdom of Osiris.

Bad souls were roasted in a fire and hacked to pieces.

Anubis was the god of the dead. He had the head of a jackal.

The body was dried out with natron, a kind of soda. Drying took about seventy days. After drying the body was washed and oiled before being wrapped tightly in linen bandages.

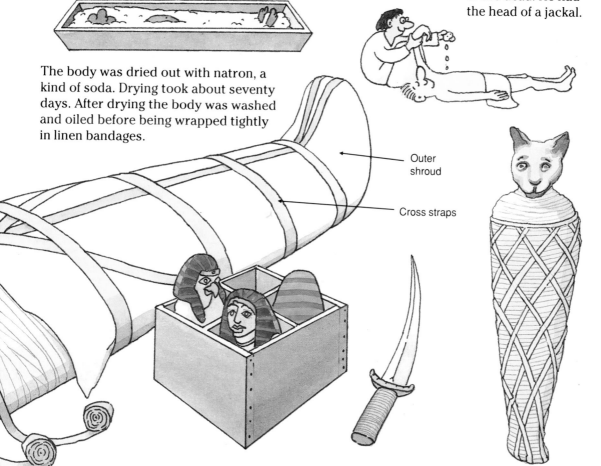

Outer shroud

Cross straps

Intestines and other organs were removed through a cut in the abdomen. The priest would plunge his arm in up to the armpit to reach to the top of the lungs. Internal organs were often kept separately in special pots called canopic jars.

Mummified cats were sacred to Bast, the goddess of pleasure.

BURIAL

If dead bodies are left lying around, they quickly rot and become a danger to health. Throughout history the commonest way to dispose of the dead has been to bury them underground. In some of the earliest graves of prehistoric Europe, stones were often laid on top of a body. It was thought that this would stop the dead from returning to haunt the living. For the same reason the feet were often tied together. Red ochre might be sprinkled on a body to represent the blood and strength it would need in an afterlife.

In modern graves there should be a depth of about six feet between the coffin lid and the surface. At the end of the funeral a few handfuls of earth are scattered on the coffin. The rest of the earth is replaced using a mechanical digger after the mourners have left.

The Vikings sometimes buried their dead under the thresholds of their houses. This was because they thought that the souls of the dead could defend their houses against evil spirits.

If a body is to be buried at sea, holes must be drilled into the coffin so that water can get in to make the coffin sink.

Other ways to dispose of bodies

The Aborigines of Australia left dead bodies in trees.

In the Solomon Islands the dead were laid out on a reef for the sharks to eat.

Tibetans have no respect for dead bodies once the soul has left them, and will even hack them to pieces for the birds to eat.

Hurry up - He's going off!

In China it is considered very important to bury a corpse in the right spot. An astrological chart with an inset compass is often used to determine the exact position and alignment for the body.

Suicide is a sin in the Christian religion. People who committed suicide were not allowed burial in Christian graveyards and were often buried at crossroads.

Fear of burial alive was widespread in the nineteenth century. A special apparatus was invented by Count Karnice-Karnicki which involved a vertical tube running from the coffin to a box above ground level. A glass sphere resting on the chest of the corpse was connected via the tube to a flag, a light and a loud bell. Any small movement of the chest would activate the mechanism.

High in the mountains of the Hindu Kush, bodies are buried upright in the snow.

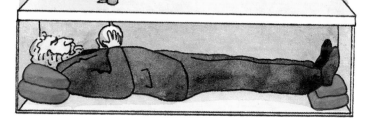

Muslims like to be buried on the same day as they die. The body should be placed on its right side, facing Mecca. On the other hand, Buddhists like to be buried facing north.

Some Inuits cover the corpse with a small igloo. Because of the cold the body will remain for ever unless it is eaten by polar bears.

The Parsees of Bombay used to leave their dead on the top of tall towers to be eaten by vultures. The vultures devour the corpses to the bone within five minutes.

GRAVEYARDS

Cemeteries are places for burial other than churchyards. Cemetery comes from the Greek word *koimeterion* which means 'dormitory'.

Christians were originally buried inside churches, not below ground.

By AD 752, many churches had become ridiculously overcrowded with dead bodies. Arms and legs sometimes stuck out of the floors and walls. So a decree from the Pope allowed graveyards to be added to churches.

However, by the seventeenth century, the same problem of overcrowding was ruining the graveyards. Between 1810 and 1830 in one graveyard in London 14,000 bodies were buried, some only two feet deep. Bones were even dug up and sold to make fertiliser.

By the nineteenth century, the case for cemeteries separate from churchyards became overwhelming. One of the first major cemeteries to be built was the Père Lachaise in Paris.

Forest Lawns Memorial Parks near Los Angeles, America, comprises four cemeteries which cover an area of two square miles. The first, established at Glendale in 1914, is home to the largest religious painting in the USA.

Emperor Constantine

The ancient Greeks and Romans used to bury their dead outside their cities. But during the Roman Empire the fashion grew for burial in underground chambers, called catacombs, within the city of Rome.

Early Christians dug catacombs beneath the church of St. Peter, the first Pope, so that they could be buried near to Peter's body. From there it was a small step to burial inside the church. The first person to be buried inside a church was the Emperor Constantine in AD 337.

In the nineteenth century, Mr Wilson of London planned to build a pyramid which would have been bigger than that of Cheops, big enough to house five million bodies. Wilson's pyramid would have been the largest cemetery ever built, but it was never completed.

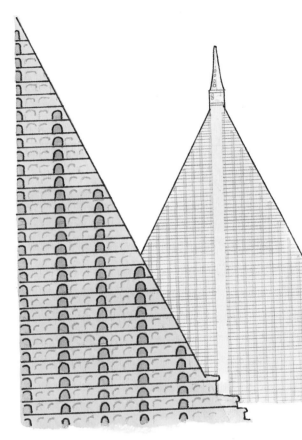

As churches became more crowded, bodies were sometimes removed from graves and placed in charnel houses.

There are thousands of bones in the charnel house of the Capuchin Church of the Immaculate Conception in Rome, arranged in complicated designs on the ceilings and walls.

To increase the popularity of the Père Lachaise cemetery, its owners dug up the bodies of famous people and reburied them there. Among the famous people reburied in this way were the playwrights Molière and Beaumarchais.

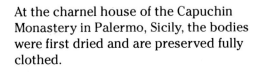

At the charnel house of the Capuchin Monastery in Palermo, Sicily, the bodies were first dried and are preserved fully clothed.

The Brookwood cemetery near Woking in Southern England was opened in 1854. A special railway, called the Brookwood Necropolis Railway, was built to carry coffins from London, sixty miles away.

The Taj Mahal is one of the seven wonders of the modern world. It was built by the Mogul Emperor Shah-Jehan for his favourite wife Arjamund Begum. Arjamund died in 1631. Work on the mausoleum started in 1632.

MEMORIALS

The earliest Christian tombstones were simple stone slabs known as ledgers. Later the ledgers were sometimes raised up on legs to form table tombs. Chest tombs were table tombs with the sides enclosed.

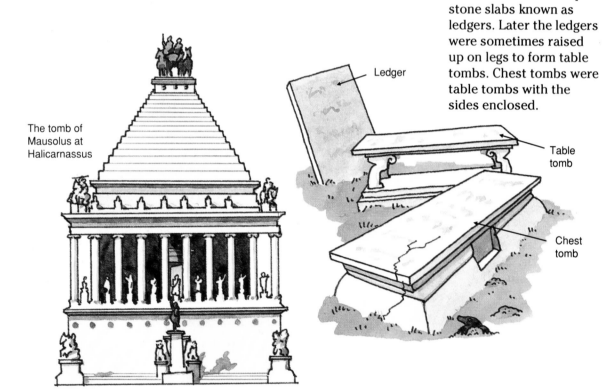

The tomb of Mausolus at Halicarnassus

Ledger

Table tomb

Chest tomb

It is human vanity to hope that we shall be remembered after we die. In many historic cultures, more money has been spent on memorials for the dead than on homes for the living. The richer and more powerful the dead person, the bigger the memorial. Mausolus was a Persian King in what is now south-western Turkey. His huge, white marble tomb at Halicarnassus was one of the Seven Wonders of the Ancient World. It was built by his wife Artemisia (who was also his sister). Artemisia mixed his ashes in wine and drank the mixture. She later joined him in their mausoleum.

It took 20,000 men working for 22 years to build the Taj Mahal.

The Emperor wanted his building to be unique. When it was finished, the hands of the craftsmen were chopped off so that they couldn't build another one like it.

Elvis Presley is buried at his home called Gracelands, in Memphis, USA, which is now an Elvis museum as well as his mausoleum.

The burial mounds of native North American Indians were sometimes built in the shapes of birds and animals. Some of these mounds were built as early as 700 BC.

Great Serpent Mound, Ohio

The tomb built for the Chinese Emperor Qin Shihuangdi was said to contain rivers of mercury. Crossbows were set to fire at grave robbers automatically. The workmen who built the tomb were walled up inside to stop them giving away the secrets of its construction.

The great pyramids are among the largest structures ever built. The pyramid of Cheops is made up of 2,500,000 blocks of stone of an average weight of 2.5 tonnes. Its height is over 140 metres and 100,000 workers took more than 20 years to build it.

The tomb of Karl Marx, the founder of communism, is in Highgate Cemetery in London.

GRAVE ROBBERS

Nowadays, to help science, many people give their bodies for medical research. Enough bodies are given each year for the researchers and medical students who need them. It wasn't always so easy. For many years, Christians believed that at the end of the world their physical bodies would be resurrected. If bodies were cut up by researchers, resurrection would be impossible.

Post-mortems were carried out by Christians in Byzantium as early as AD 50. In Parma in 1286, bodies were cut open to try to discover the cause of the plague. These were exceptions. Even as late as 1380, Pope Boniface banned the boiling or cutting up of corpses. It was only during the Renaissance that dissection was permitted in Europe. Even then, it was only allowed on the bodies of executed criminals.

There was always a shortage of bodies. And the shortage grew worse with the growth of medical schools in the eighteenth century. Medical students needed bodies to practise on. Grave robbers, or resurrectionists, stepped in to supply the bodies.

Grave robbing made easy

Dig a vertical shaft to the head of the coffin.

Cover with sacking to reduce the noise.

Prise off the coffin lid.

Haul out the body using a noose tied round the neck.

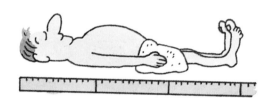

Children's bodies were often sold by the foot: six shillings for the first foot and nine pence per inch thereafter.

The Crouch gang was one of the most famous gangs of grave robbers. They operated in London in the early 1800s.

This picture is taken from *The Resurrectionists* by the cartoonist Thomas Rowlandson (1756-1827).

William Harvey, who discovered that blood circulates round the body, dissected the dead bodies of his own father and sister.

In the sixteenth century, the French government gave one criminal per year to the medical profession for live dissection. Live dissection was also practised by Greek doctors in ancient Alexandria.

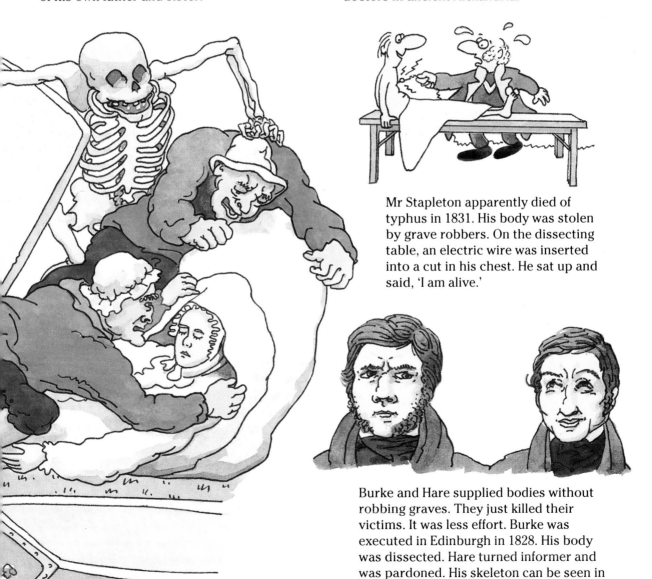

Mr Stapleton apparently died of typhus in 1831. His body was stolen by grave robbers. On the dissecting table, an electric wire was inserted into a cut in his chest. He sat up and said, 'I am alive.'

Burke and Hare supplied bodies without robbing graves. They just killed their victims. It was less effort. Burke was executed in Edinburgh in 1828. His body was dissected. Hare turned informer and was pardoned. His skeleton can be seen in the anatomy museum at Edinburgh University.

GRAVE GOODS

The custom of burying things with the dead is at least 60,000 years old. The rich and powerful were buried with treasure, and even with their servants. Ordinary people were buried with food and drink and sometimes cups and tools. Things may have been buried with dead bodies because it was believed that they would be useful in the after-life. Much of what we know about ancient people has been learned from studying their grave goods.

The tomb of the Qin Emperor of China contained an army of life-sized clay soldiers and the bodies of all his concubines who were killed specially for his burial.

Some Bronze Age people only buried a dead person's skull with a few possessions.

In ancient China, jaw bones of pigs were buried with the dead.

The Egyptian pyramids were like palaces stuffed with treasures. The tomb of Tutankhamun contained the largest hoard of ancient golden artefacts ever found.

Neanderthal graves 60,000 years old have been found containing the remains of flowers.

The Egyptian queen Her-Neith was buried with her favourite dog.

A thirteenth century Maharajah of Jaipur was buried with his favourite elephant.

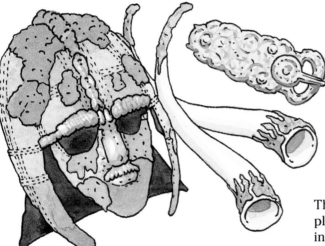

In India, a Mogul prince was buried with his barber.

The Adena tribe of Ohio placed clay tobacco pipes in graves, in case the dead should wish to smoke.

The burial ship of a Saxon king dating from AD 650 was found at Sutton Hoo. It contained some of the richest treasures ever found in England.

In the Middle Ages, consecrated bread was buried in the grave, so that the dead could offer it to God. Priests were buried with a cross and a cup as well as the bread.

The royal tombs of ancient Sumeria had running water so that the dead could drink.

Nowadays, if children die, their favourite toys may be buried with them.

Among other things, the ancient Celts would put games in the grave so that the dead would have something to amuse themselves with in the next world.

23

RELICS

The remains of bodies often have been thought to have magical powers. The cannibals of Melanesia used to eat the bodies of their enemies, not for the meat, but in order to aquire the strength of their victims. They said the meat tasted of pork. They called the flesh of missionaries 'long pig'.

The bones of Christian saints are still thought by many to have miraculous powers, and pilgrims travel long distances to see them. Arm, leg and head bones are considered the most holy. In the Middle Ages, these holy relics were big business. Pilgrims had money to spend, just like tourists today. Bones were often divided up. John the Baptist's went to Amiens, Rhodes, Besançon and several other places. Today such beliefs are less common.

St Hugh of Lincoln bit off two pieces of Mary Magdelene's arm bone when on a pilgrimage to Normandy, and smuggled them back to England.

A Buddhist ritual trumpet made from a human thigh bone.

Food facts

Leave a toe for me!

Not only the Melanesians ate human flesh. Some aboriginal Australian tribes ate the flesh of dead relatives as a mark of respect.

Dinner's nearly ready!

In some parts of Indonesia the liquids of a decomposing body were mixed with rice and eaten. It was believed that this food had magical properties.

Careful with Grandad's head son!

On some islands of Melanesia the skull of the deceased is given to a near relative to use as a drinking cup.

One of the vertebrae of the astronomer Galileo was stolen in 1757. It is now displayed in Padua.

One of the holiest shrines of Buddhism is the Temple of the Tooth at Kandy in Sri Lanka, where Buddha's left canine tooth is kept.

The ancient Celts hung the heads of their enemies from their horses and outside their houses.

A hair from the beard of the Prophet Mohammed is preserved in resin in the Topkapi museum in Istanbul.

Frederich Ruysh (1638-1731) made tableaux from the skeletons of children together with preserved parts of the human body and stuffed birds. His collection was bought by Peter the Great of Russia.

CREMATION

In AD 789, Emperor Charlemagne decreed death for anyone practising cremation. Cremation was considered unchristian because it was thought that a burned body could not be resurrected at the Last Judgement.

The first cremations in the USA were carried out in Washington in 1876, in the private crematorium of a doctor, Julius Lemogne. In Britain, the first legal cremation took place in 1883 when Dr William Price, an 83 year old Welsh druidic priest, cremated his five month old baby, whom he had named Jesus Christ Price.

Modern crematoriums reduce a body to ashes in about one and a half hours. The newest models working at temperatures up to 1,200 degrees centigrade are even quicker. Wood ash from the coffin is light, and goes up the chimney together with any water vapour, leaving the bones and the ashes of the body behind. Any metal, for instance gold from teeth, is collected from the ashes. Finally, the bone fragments are crushed to a fine powder in a special machine. The final residue per adult weighs about three kilograms. This is collected into a tin can with a screw top, ready to be emptied into an urn or to be scattered.

An early crematorium

The Beaker people who lived in Europe around 4,000 years ago used to collect the ashes of their dead in beakers or decorated pots.

Suttee was a cruel tradition common in India until banned by the British in 1829. Widows were expected to burn alive with their dead husbands, sometimes cradling their husband's head on their laps and lighting the fire themselves. In 1780, when Rajah Ajit Singh was cremated, sixty-four of his wives were burned alive with him.

Gypsy kings and queens are burned in their caravans.

Os resectum is a mixture of burial and cremation. A finger is cut off and buried, while the rest of the body is burned. The buried finger is the seed for the new body which will be resurrected on judgement day.

Viking leaders were placed in their favourite long boat, which was then set alight and pushed out to sea.

The poet Percy Bysshe Shelley drowned off the coast of Italy in 1822. His body was burned on an open fire on the beach. Wine, incense and oil were thrown on to the flames. Trelawney, his friend, plucked the heart from the fire, badly burning his own hand. The heart was returned to England in a box.

Nowadays, cremation is forbidden for orthodox Jews, Parsees, Muslims and Greek Orthodox Christians. Hindus always cremate their dead. The eldest son lights the funeral pyre.

LIFE AFTER DEATH

Most people throughout history have believed that their spirit continues to live after their mortal body is dead, although there has always been a minority of atheists who do not believe in God and think that when you're dead you're dead.

The ancient Mesopotamians believed that the souls of the dead fell into a huge pit called the 'Land of No Return'.

The Vikings believed that the souls of warriors who died in battle went to a life of feasting in Valhalla, the hall of the god Odin.

The ancient Celts believed that the afterworld was a place of happiness where they could indulge in all their favourite activities. There would be lots to eat and drink and plenty of fighting, and wounds would heal overnight. For this reason the Celts did not fear death and often went into battle naked.

Christians believe that the good go to Heaven and the bad go to Hell. However, there may be a long time to wait until Judgement Day. Because Hell is such a severe punishment, most Christians believe that the dead go to be purified before being admitted to heaven. This stage of purification is called purgatory and can be thought of as a temporary hell.

I tell you these are not just beans - they are human beans!

Rubbish!

Pull the other one.

Who do you want to be when you grow up?

Pythagoras!

Pythagoras, the ancient Greek philosopher, believed that broad beans contained the souls of the dead so he forbade his followers to eat them.

Hindus and Buddhists believe that the soul experiences many lives. After death the soul is reborn in a new young body which can be an animal or a person. This is called reincarnation. Eventually very good, wise people can escape the cycle of reincarnation and enter into a state of one-ness with the universe called nirvana.

The Aborigines believe that their spirits exist before and after life in a state called Dreamtime. The spirits of the tribe and of its special animals are reborn again and again.

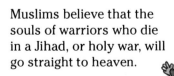

Muslims believe that the souls of warriors who die in a Jihad, or holy war, will go straight to heaven.

The Greek underworld was a grey place of shadows called the Kingdom of Hades. Dead people were pale shadows of their former selves. Hades was guarded by a giant three-headed dog called Cerberus and surrounded by the river Styx. A corner of Hades called Elysium was slightly more pleasant and was reserved for heroes.

Cryonics is a method of freeze drying bodies in the hope that they can be thawed out and brought back to life in the future. People ask for this treatment because they believe that a cure for the cause of their death may be discovered in the future.

Hurry up dear! The ice is melting!

After death the body must be connected immediately to a heart-lung machine and packed in water ice.

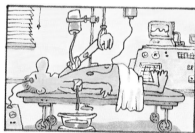

Later the blood is drained out of the body, and replaced with preservative fluid.

DEEP FROZEN FUTURE

The population of the world is now 5,000 million people and it's still growing. About 5 million tonnes of dead bodies have to be disposed of every year. The problems of disposal are going to increase in the future.

Cryonics poses many problems. In particular, would future generations want to revive thousands of frozen bodies?

Millions of bodies were mummified in ancient Egypt. If it were possible for us to revive them, would we want all those ancient Egyptians to look after?

In the USA today some people pay up to $150,000 to be mummified after death using techniques based on those of the ancient Egyptians.

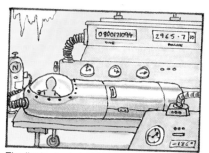

Finally the body is frozen in liquid nitrogen. Keeping it frozen is very expensive.

Are you dead yet?

Nearly!

It's unlikely that cryonics is effective. To really work, bodies should be frozen before they die.

The first dead body to be permanently frozen was James Bedford, a Californian teacher of psychology, in 1967.

Quick drying may be used in future to preserve bodies for later revival. In 1954 the body of a ten year old Inca prince was discovered in a cave on a mountain near Santiago, Chile. The child had died 500 years before but the body had been very well preserved in the cold, dry air.

The frozen bodies of mammoths have been found in the ice of Siberia. Their meat could still be eaten after thousands of years. In the future people may consider it wasteful to burn or bury 5 million tonnes of nutritious dead bodies every year. They could be frozen and eaten instead!

INDEX

First published in 1993 by
Watts Books
96 Leonard Street
London EC2A 4RH

Paperback edition 1994

10 9 8 7 6 5 4 3 2 1

Franklin Watts Australia
14 Mars Road
Lane Cove
NSW 2060

© 1993 Lazy Summer Books Ltd
Illustrated by Lazy Summer Books Ltd

UK ISBN 0 7496 1186 3 (hardback)
UK ISBN 0 7496 1596 6 (paperback)

A CIP catalogue record for this book is
available from the British Library
Dewey Decimal Classification: 393

Printed in Belgium

PRINTED IN BELGIUM BY
proost
INTERNATIONAL BOOK PRODUCTION

LEIGHTON HOUSE MUSEUM · HOLLAND PARK ROAD · KENSINGTON

Daniel Robbins

Leighton House Museum
Holland Park Road, Kensington

The Royal Borough of Kensington and Chelsea
Culture Service

Published by The Royal Borough of Kensington and Chelsea

Leighton House Museum · 12 Holland Park Road · London W14 8LZ
Telephone 020 7602 3316 · www.rbkc.gov.uk/leightonhousemuseum

ISBN 0 902242 23 7

Text by Daniel Robbins, *Senior Curator, Museums*
The first edition of this guide in 2005 was dedicated to my
grandparents. All have since passed away. This is dedicated to their
memory and to their great-grandsons, Luc, Edgar and Gabriel.

Copy photography by John Rogers
Edited by Perilla Kinchin
Picture Research by Philippa Martin and Rebecca Jallot

Designed and typeset in Manticore by Dalrymple
Printed in Belgium by DeckersSnoeck

Front cover: The south elevation, Leighton House
(photo Martin Charles)
Frontispiece. The staircase hall (photo Will Pryce)
Back cover: The Arab Hall (photo Will Pryce)
Endpapers: Detail of a late sixteenth-century tile panel from
Damascus, Syria, installed on the west wall of the Arab Hall
(photo John Rogers)

Contents

Foreword

The Royal Borough of Kensington and Chelsea has always been a popular place to live and work amongst artists, writers and musicians and continues to be so today. It is also home to an unrivalled collection of museums. These two strands come together in Leighton House Museum. Built as a private residence by the eminent Victorian artist Frederic Leighton, it has been open as a museum since 1900 and in the care of the Royal Borough since 1927. No other purpose-built artist's studio-house is open to the public in the UK. Together with its sister museum, Linley Sambourne House at 18 Stafford Terrace, Leighton House provides visitors from all over the world with a glimpse of the wealth and status enjoyed by Victorian artists and represents an important part of the history of the Royal Borough.

In October 2008, the museum closed for a £1.6 million programme of restoration and refurbishment funded by the Council. This investment has secured the future of the building and brought the presentation of the interiors closer to Leighton's original decorative schemes than at any time in the past century.

The house reopened in April 2010 and the Council hopes that this new edition of the guidebook, updated to reflect the changes made through the restoration project, will encourage greater understanding and appreciation of this wonderful house and its collections.

COUNCILLOR NICHOLAS PAGET-BROWN
Deputy Leader and Cabinet Member for Transportation, Environment and Leisure

SUPPORTERS AND DONORS

The Heritage Lottery Fund for support of projects and acquisitions

The Art Fund and the V&A/MLA Purchase Grant Fund for their support of acquisitions for the permanent collections.

The restoration of the staircase hall and Narcissus Hall in 2000 was generously supported by John Schaeffer.

The copies of Corot's *The Four Times of the Day* for the drawing room were made in 2009–10 with the support of The Grocers Company and a private donor.

Mr Essie Sakhai, Essie Carpets, for the generous loan of carpets for display in the house.

The Friends of Leighton House Museum and 18 Stafford Terrace

George Frederic Watts (1817–1904)
Portrait of Frederic Leighton, 1871

Purchased in 2004 with the support of the Heritage Lottery Fund, the Art Fund, the V&A/MLA Purchase Funds, the Friends of Leighton House Museum and Linley Sambourne House, and private donations.
LH 2183

Introduction

1 *Previous pages: Leighton House Museum seen from the garden.*

2 *Leighton in his studio, c.1890. On the easel is the portrait of his sister Alexandra now in the museum's collections (see pl.34, cat.no.70).*

He built his house as it now stands for his own artistic delight. Every stone of it had been the object of his loving care. It was a joy to him until the moment when he lay down to die.

LEIGHTON'S SISTERS IN A LETTER TO THE TIMES, 26 JANUARY 1899

Leighton House is inextricably linked to the life of its one and only occupant, Frederic Leighton. It was built entirely to his requirements; he was closely involved in its design, construction and decoration and wholly responsible for the collections of fine and decorative art that filled it. The house evolved in tandem with his career: it was relatively modest in its first incarnation, completed in 1866 just two years after Leighton became an Associate of the Royal Academy. By the time of his death thirty years later as the Academy's newly ennobled President, the house had become his extraordinary private Palace of Art.

While Leighton's was not quite the first purpose-built studio-house in Britain, he was the first British artist really to understand the part such a house could play in the furtherance of a reputation and career. It was carefully conceived to balance private, public and professional considerations. Here he could live as well as work and entertain in an environment that made plain his obvious though unostentatious wealth, his devotion to art, and his discerning taste and connoisseurship. The decision to build was itself a statement of intent, a means of establishing an immediate 'presence' in London's artistic society. Regularly featured in the press and opened to an eager public on 'Show Sundays', Leighton's house played a significant part in defining what it was to be an eminent artist in the late Victorian period.

At the centre of it all was Leighton himself. Handsome and cosmopolitan, his elegant appearance, sophisticated manner and apparently effortless command of five languages allowed him to move in the highest social circles. His contribution to public life and in particular his presidency of the Royal Academy between 1878 and 1896 won unanimous praise and respect. He became 'the visible embodiment to the world of English art'. He was exceptionally generous and supportive towards friends who needed help and remained close to his sisters Alexandra and Augusta throughout his life. But he could also appear a remote, distant figure. While he was a renowned and regular host, his house contained no guest accommodation. He never married and lived entirely alone but for his staff. In later life he certainly felt constrained by the demands of his position and his many obligations. Some were evidently suspicious of his social charm and princely manner, sensing that these qualities deflected real intimacy and candour. Following his death, 'Mercutio' observed, 'his acquaintances were legion; he was admired and respected by all; his charities were boundless; but who probed beneath that detached personality? He was always alone, and yet he was never solitary.'

Research has uncovered circumstantial evidence that in 1875 Leighton may have fathered a child by one of his models, Lily Mason. His relationship with Dorothy Dene, his model and muse for the last years of his life was also profound. Perhaps in simple terms Leighton had reasons for keeping his private life very private. The part that his house played in creating and then maintaining his public persona, while at the same time allowing his complex personality to remain hidden, is one of its many fascinations.

The fortunes of the house following Leighton's death continued to mirror his reputation. Immediately considered worthy of saving for the nation, it later slipped into neglect and misuse. From the early 1980s a programme of restoration began the slow transformation of the house. Progressively, each of the interiors was returned to something approaching its original appearance and this process continued through the 1990s and into the new century. The major refurbishment project completed between 2008 and 2010 allowed for the comprehensive re-presentation of the house and the introduction of additional furnishings and objects, building on the research and findings of the earlier restorations.

Frederic Leighton 1830–1896

What I admire in him is that he never ceases to strive after perfection even in the minutest details; and I admire this all the more because he is in a fair way to be spoilt by attention and flattery.

JOSEPH JOACHIM, 1876

Frederic Leighton was born at 13 Brunswick Terrace, Scarborough, Yorkshire on 3 December 1830, the second of three children of Dr Frederic Septimus Leighton and Augusta Susan Nash. The family moved to London in 1833 and Leighton subsequently attended University College School. In 1841, for the sake of his mother's health, the family began spending extended periods on the continent. Leighton's grandfather, James, had also been a doctor. He emigrated to St Petersburg in 1805–6 and rose to become Physician to Their Imperial Majesties of All the Russias and Physician-General to the Imperial Fleet. He was knighted at the request of the Czar in 1830, and also rewarded with a sizeable personal fortune. Sir James's death in 1843 left Leighton's father wealthy enough to have little need to practise medicine. He lived to be ninety-two, predeceasing Leighton by just four years and providing him with a private income throughout this time. Travel remained a constant theme of Leighton's life, with weeks and sometimes months spent overseas each year.

At an early age Leighton had shown an interest in drawing. As the family travelled, he enrolled for brief periods at the Berlin Academy of Art and the Academia delle Belle Arti in Florence. In 1846 the Leightons set up home in Frankfurt and Frederic began his formal art training at the Städelsches Kunstinstitut, an indication that his father's initial scepticism about his chosen career had been overcome. Here Leighton was taught by Edward von Steinle (1810–86), the Nazarene painter whom he came to regard as his single greatest influence. In 1848, political unrest forced the Leightons to leave the city and they spent two years first in Brussels and then Paris, before returning to Frankfurt. In 1852 the family finally returned to England, taking up permanent residence in Bath.

Leighton remained on the continent. Following the completion of his studies he travelled to Rome, where he spent the next three years producing the works to launch his career as a painter. After an uncertain start, it became a carefree period of great personal and artistic fulfilment. Friendships were established that would be sustained for the rest of Leighton's life and his engaging personality, allied to a drive and ambition that would carry him to the top of his profession, became increasingly evident. The principal product of this time was the vast canvas, *Cimabue's Celebrated Madonna is Carried in Procession through the Streets of Florence*. Exhibited at the Royal Academy in 1855 it was immediately bought by Queen Victoria and the previously unknown Leighton

was widely identified as the great hope of English painting.

With this success behind him, in the autumn of 1855 Leighton travelled to Paris for the final leg of his artistic education. Taking a studio in rue Pigalle, he mixed with the British expatriate community and met many of the city's prominent artists, including Ingres and Delacroix. He befriended several others such as Alexandre-Gabriel Decamps and Constant Troyon. However, *The Triumph of Music*, his follow-up to *Cimabue*, was very poorly received on exhibition at the Royal Academy in 1856. Nothing was shown the following year: the meteoric success of Leighton's debut evidently cast a long shadow.

After a last winter in Rome, Leighton returned to London in 1859, finally settling in the country where he had not lived for any length of time since his earliest childhood. Fluent in French, German, Italian and Spanish, he had a richness of experience and cultural sophistication that marked him out from his contemporaries. At the same time, the evidence of a 'foreign' training was the source of some prejudice amongst critics and contemporaries, even after his election as an Associate of the Royal Academy in 1864. In the same year he commissioned the studio-house in Holland Park Road where he would live until his death. His reputation continued to grow with a series of impressive works exhibited at the Academy through the mid 1860s. *The Syracusan Bride* (1866) marked a transition from the medieval subjects of his early

career to the classical themes dominant in his mature years. In 1868 he was elected a full Academician and began to play an increasing role in the life of the institution, serving on committees and assisting in the organisation of the annual winter exhibitions. Leighton's increasing prominence was recognised by a private visit from Queen Victoria on 12 March 1869, after which she noted in her Journal: 'He is most agreeable & gentlemanlike, & his house & studio charmingly arranged ...'.

In 1878, Leighton was elected President of the Royal Academy and knighted. He was appointed President of the International Jury on Paintings at the Exposition Universelle in Paris in the same year and made Officier de la Légion d'Honneur, the first of numerous international honours. Leighton proved an extremely effective President, displaying great administrative and diplomatic skill in handling the Academicians and making particular efforts to draw into the institution artists such as his friends G.F. Watts and Edward Burne-Jones, who were by temperament inclined to remain outside. Leighton increasingly used his wealth and public stature to support a variety of causes and campaigns that he considered would enhance the cultural life of the nation.

The energy with which Leighton continued to work, combined with his many public duties and social commitments, began to take a toll on his health from the late 1880s. In October 1894, he suffered a first attack of angina. Advised to absent himself from

Academy duties, Leighton spent much of 1895 abroad, in North Africa in the spring and on a final trip to Italy in the autumn. On 22 December 1895, the Prime Minister, Lord Salisbury, wrote to Leighton offering him a peerage. He was created Baron Leighton of Stretton in the New Year's Honours List, the first artist to be recognised in this way. He did not enjoy this public tribute for long: on 25 January 1896 he died at home.

Leighton's coffin lay first in the studio at his house and was then taken to the Royal Academy. With the express approval of Queen Victoria, he was buried with great ceremony in St Paul's Cathedral on 3 February 1896.

The Building of 2 Holland Park Road

6 *George Aitchison's presentation drawing of the Silk Room, April 1895.*

7 *A page of architectural drawings, probably in Venice, from one of Leighton's sketchbooks.*

'I wish I had a house', wrote Frederic Leighton to his mother in 1862. Since returning to England in 1859, he had been living in rented accommodation at 2 Orme Square, Bayswater. A visit by bailiffs seeking unpaid taxes from his landlord and threatening to remove Leighton's own furniture as payment, gave added urgency to what had evidently been a long-held desire. The American sculptress Harriet Hosmer recalled how she and Leighton discussed the matter in Rome in 1858: 'Leighton described to me the house he would build "as soon" said he "as I am able to pay for it".' After dinner he proceeded to sketch out the intended plan of the house 'in every respect as it was afterwards executed'. Whether or not this took place quite as described, from an early stage in his career Leighton clearly intended to build rather than purchase a house, and meant to be closely involved in its realisation.

Architecture was a deep and abiding interest for Leighton. By the early 1860s he had already travelled widely through continental Europe and into North Africa, motivated as much by a desire to see and study architecture as by more painterly concerns. His sketchbooks include many precisely rendered architectural subjects and detailed notes and sketches of capitals, mouldings and profiles. He amassed a substantial architectural library and counted architects, not least the architect of his own house, George Aitchison, among his closest friends. Much later, in 1894, Leighton was the first artist to be awarded the Royal Institute of British

Architects' Gold Medal in recognition of 'the clearest evidence of his potential merit had he had occasion to practise in our special branch'.

In addition to an excellent general architectural knowledge Leighton also brought to bear an expertise in the challenge of combining house and painting studio, the product of the time he had spent living and working on the continent through the 1850s. For three years in Paris Leighton rented a studio in the rue Pigalle, an area heavily populated by artists and including several studio-houses. Contacts with new friends and colleagues gave many opportunities for absorbing various combinations of living and working arrangements. He certainly visited Eugène Delacroix's house and purpose-built studio, and that of Ary Scheffer, whose musical parties in his artistically appointed studio were a model for the gatherings Leighton later devised. Before Paris, the three formative years Leighton spent in Rome between 1852 and 1855 provided their own insights. The role that the studio could play as a venue for entertainment and gatherings among a community of artists and sculptors took an early hold on his imagination.

By 1864 Leighton was beginning to enjoy the financial and professional status that could make a reality of his intentions. In the summer he was elected an Associate of the Royal Academy and in August sold his *Dante in Exile* for £1,050, considerably more than anything he had yet realised for a painting. His income continued to rise through 1865 and 1866 with several substantial sales: *The*

Syracusan Bride sold for £1,200 in 1866. Most importantly, an ideal site had become available. Leighton wrote to his father in the summer of 1864:

> I should not leave the place that I am in except to build; a mended house would be most unsatisfactory and *temporary*. I feel sure I shall get nowhere standing room for a house for less than £28 (per annum), still less room for a house and *large garden*. If I find the terms exactly as I suspect ... I shall, I think, close the bargain.

The Site: Little Holland House

Leighton's plot was on Holland Park Road, a lane on the southern edge of the Holland Estate. The south side of the road was bordered by the back gardens and stable

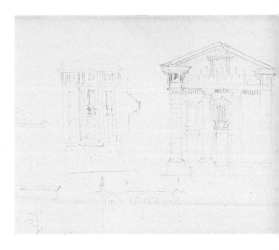

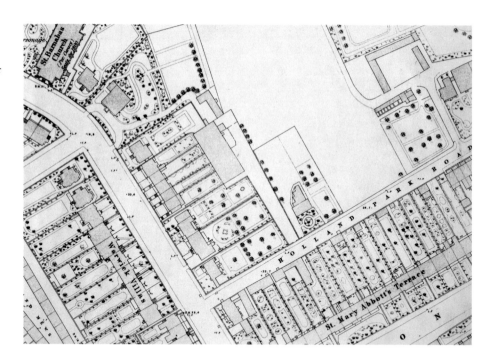

buildings of St Mary Abbott's Terrace, built in the late 1820s. There was also development to the west, with private villas along Addison Road, but the setting retained a distinctly rural feel. North of the site was uninterrupted parkland and the only building in the immediate vicinity was Holland Farm, still a going concern complete with cowsheds and piggeries, just to the east. Beyond it, a little further to the north-east was Little Holland House, a charming old house in a large garden that served as the dower house to the nearby Jacobean mansion of Holland House itself. Much of the appeal of Leighton's site was bound up with the remarkable household then in residence at Little Holland House.

In 1855 Leighton had met the painter George Frederic Watts. Although he was some thirteen years Leighton's senior, their friendship was particularly close and would remain so for the next forty years. Watts was living as a long-term houseguest of Thoby and Sara Prinsep who, at his suggestion, had taken the lease on Little Holland House from Lord and Lady Holland in 1850. Watts had met and become friends with the Hollands in Florence in 1843. Thoby Prinsep was a retired Indian civil servant and his wife Sara was one of the seven Pattle sisters (another was the photographer Julia Margaret Cameron). With Watts as its star attraction and the Pattle sisters as an additional draw, the house with its slightly bohemian and highly cultivated residents became a magnet for artists, writers and

politicians. The young Edward Burne-Jones retreated there to recover from illness, and amongst the many visitors was Leighton.

The financial circumstances of the Holland family had for some time been precarious. Gradually parts of the estate were being sold off for development. Leighton, perhaps with Watts' encouragement, was perfectly placed to open negotiations with Lady Holland or gain early notice of the release of further plots. In September 1864 a deal was complete and Leighton could start planning in earnest. He was not alone in seeking to build a studio-house. With help from his parents, Valentine Prinsep, Thoby and Sara's artist son, had secured the ground immediately to the west of Leighton's. Both plots measured 28.75 × 43.33m allowing for gardens narrower and considerably shorter than those which the owners ultimately enjoyed. Both artists gained permission for the construction of stable blocks and summerhouses at the end of their respective gardens, although these

were never carried out. Leighton added a strip of land to the east of his house in 1868, sublet from the neighbouring farm. In the mid 1870s when Melbury Road was constructed and the land along it sold to a new set of artists for the construction of studio-houses, both Leighton and Prinsep took the opportunity to extend their plots to the north, to keep their new neighbours at a distance with substantial gardens. (Prinsep, in fact, sublet the end of his garden to Watts for the construction of his studio-house, Little Holland House – the old Little Holland House was demolished in 1875). The buildings went up together, with Prinsep's completed a few months ahead of Leighton's in 1866. They remained close friends and neighbours until Leighton's death.

Prinsep's house was designed by Philip Webb, who had completed the Red House at Bexleyheath for William Morris in 1860. He would become the leading domestic architect of the Arts and Crafts Movement. Leighton's architect had less of a pedigree.

The Architect: George Aitchison

9 *George Aitchison, Leighton's architect, photographed in 1898.*

10 *Sketch of the fireplace elevation in the dining room, contained in one of Leighton's sketchbooks, c.1865.*

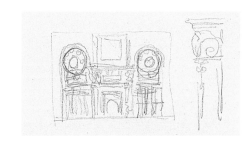

George Aitchison was born in London on 7 November 1825 and 'bred in an architectural atmosphere'. His father, also George Aitchison, was architect to the St Katherine Dock Company and a designer of stations on the London and Birmingham Railway. After leaving Merchant Taylors' School, Aitchison was articled to his father and in 1853, as many young architects did, set off on a continental tour. In Rome he met the artist George Hemming Mason who introduced him to the 22-year-old Leighton. Leighton was at work on his great canvas, *Cimabue's Celebrated Madonna is Carried in Procession Through the Streets of Florence*.

Aitchison, five years older, later recalled modelling a sleeve for the figure of Cimabue in his new friend's painting. At Leighton's suggestion, in the spring of 1854 he left Rome with the architect William Burges on a tour of Italy that took them to Arezzo, Perugia and Assisi, and then to Florence for several months. Retreating from a cholera epidemic, they then travelled through France before separating. Aitchison travelled further in Italy with his parents before finally returning to England in 1855.

On his return, Aitchison started work in earnest with his father, becoming his partner in 1859 and succeeding him on his death in 1861. The practice was almost entirely concerned with building wharves, warehouses and railway works, often on a vast scale. Aitchison's daily work could not have been further removed from the commissions that would later make his name, but he had always numbered artists and sculptors amongst his closest friends. In the early 1860s Leighton would apparently call at the Aitchison family home and insist on 'having a dance with Aitchison's sisters and other girl friends', and, in 1864 he commissioned his 'old friend' to design his studio-house.

Prior to Leighton's commission Aitchison had designed no domestic buildings at all, but the house would remain a constant part of his professional life for the next thirty years. Through Leighton's patronage, a whole new set of clients and commissions opened up. Leighton's remained the only house that he built outright: it was principally as the designer of

highly decorative and beautifully coloured interiors for wealthy and influential clients that Aitchison's career now developed. These included interiors for James Stewart Hodgson, one of Leighton's most loyal patrons, at his house in South Audley Street, Mayfair (for which Leighton contributed two painted friezes, see pl.113, cat. nos.62, 63) and his country house at Lythe Hill, Surrey. He also completed work for the artists G.F. Watts (building a picture gallery onto his house in Melbury Road), and Lawrence Alma Tadema. In 1878 he carried out the decoration of the British Art Section at the Paris Exhibition – Leighton was the chairman of the Paintings Jury.

These commissions stemmed from Aitchison's friendship with Leighton and the house they had created together. The relationship was rooted in their shared experience of Rome and the common interests and enthusiasms revealed there. Crucially, Leighton must have known his friend would not resist his close involvement in every aspect of the design of the house. To this extent, Aitchison's relative inexperience was a positive advantage. It may never be possible to determine the precise degree of Leighton's involvement, but it is safe to assume it was substantial. A sketchbook of Leighton's dating from 1865–6 includes a rough sketch for the east wall of the dining room and sketch plans of the drawing room and bedroom, the former indicating where he proposed to place his furniture. Edgcumbe Staley reported Aitchison as stating that 'every stone, every brick – even

11 *The house as first completed, as illustrated in the Building News, 1866.*

12 *Plans of the house as first built taken from those published in the Building News.*

mortar and the cement – no less than all the wood and metal work passed directly under his (Leighton's) personal observation.'

At the same time, Leighton's Coutts bank account reveals the extent of Aitchison's involvement in the development of the house. The first recorded payment to him is in September 1865 and on Leighton's death in January 1896, Aitchison is listed amongst his creditors, owed £60 for the recently completed construction of the Silk Room. In the thirty years between, Aitchison is paid at least once in every year with the exception of just five. Average yearly payments were in excess of £100. No other architect is recorded as having any input into the house throughout its many extensions and redecorations.

The First Phase of Construction: 1865–7

Work on the house started in the second half of 1865. The builders were William Hack & Son of Poplar, who were paid a total of £3,763. Around November, Leighton went abroad for the winter, entrusting Aitchison with £1000 and leaving him to supervise construction. According to Staley, before departing Leighton 'bound Aitchison and all others who were concerned in the building and fitting of the house and studio to carry out his instructions implicitly. These included the minutest directions about the shape, size and decoration of the furniture, which Aitchison was called upon

to design specifically.' Building continued throughout 1866. Again Leighton felt able to leave the work in Aitchison's hands, travelling that year through Spain on a 'prolonged stay'. In October he was in Rome and on his return the house was sufficiently complete for him to move in. Mrs Kendall, his first housekeeper, appears to have taken up her position in the same month, and in November the house was featured in the *Building News*. In later years there would be a steady stream of reviews and articles in the press. Work almost certainly continued into the first few months of 1867: the garden was landscaped by Lee & Son of Hammersmith, who continued to maintain it with its lawn of 'velvet-like grass' up to the time of Leighton's death.

When first completed, 2 Holland Park Road, as it was known, was relatively modest in size. Leighton's father had cautioned his son about the likely expense and it is clear that the project did stretch his resources. He committed to doing 'nothing without an

estimate', and with Aitchison he conceived a first phase of building that could be extended as resources allowed. This had the added advantage of allowing him to keep options open as to what accommodation an extension might contain. He did confess that 'I shall probably be obliged to build at once rather more than I absolutely require for practical building reasons', and argued that some allowance had to be made for the particular requirements of 'an artist who lives by his eyes'. In 1865 with construction underway, he wrote to the archaeologist and collector, Henry Layard that 'I have found the expense of my housebuilding grow so much – I am obliged to exercise an amount of circumspection in my expenditure which I have hitherto not practised.' Part of that expenditure had been on paintings, furniture and artefacts, and it is clear that the new house was in certain instances planned around works already in his possession. The subsequent extensions also responded to the display of particular art works. The entire cost of this

THE STUDIO

GALLERY

MODEL'S ACCESS
TO STUDIO AND
SERVICE STAIRCASE

DRESSING/
BATH ROOM

BEDROOM

13 The first extension to the house of 1869–70 was supported by a loggia on the ground floor. The position of the large new canvas store is indicated by the circular windows in the east and south elevations. Building News, 1880.

ARTISTS' · HOMES · Nº 7 · Sᴵᴿ Fredᵏ Leighton P.RᴬA · House & Studio · Kensington

George Aitchison BᴬA.

ARCHITECT

first phase was given as £4,500, a substantial amount for that time.

The exterior of the building was strikingly plain and devoid of obvious stylistic references. This may have been partly due to budgetary limitations, but Aitchison and Leighton both wrote of their preference for the avoidance of historical style. The main entrance was placed at the left of the front façade, with the apparent intention that a later extension would create a symmetrical arrangement around the front door. The whole building was pressed up against the street, maximising the garden area at the rear. The east elevation was plain and functional while the north façade onto the garden was dominated by the large studio window on the first floor.

Internally, the staircase hall occupied a dominant central position in the L-shaped plan. From here there was access to the drawing room and dining room on the north side of the building and the breakfast room overlooking the street. On the first

floor were Leighton's small and surprisingly austere bedroom, his bathroom and the grand painting studio. The kitchens and servants' rooms were in the basement, with two servants' bedrooms the only accommodation on the top floor.

The First Extension: 1869–70

Within three years of Leighton's moving in, substantial works were again underway – not the planned additions to the west of the original block, but an extension of the east end of the studio on the first floor. These works probably never formed part of a master plan, but were prompted by practical shortcomings in the operation of the studio. According to Aitchison, the extension, which involved dismantling its entire east wall and building on an additional 4.5m was required to accommodate 'some big canvases', but it also addressed the problems of access arrangements for models and a shortage of storage space.

Work started towards the end of 1869, coinciding with Leighton's departure abroad, and was probably completed in the late spring of 1870. The builders Longmire & Burge of East Street, Manchester Square, were paid £500. In contrast to the four or five works Leighton typically submitted to the Royal Academy each year, only one minor painting was shown in 1870, evidence of the disruption of his studio, coupled with the effects of rheumatism contracted in December 1869.

The Arab Hall Extension: 1877–81

The period from 1872 to 1876 saw no major works to the house. Aitchison was paid nothing in 1874 or 1875, although Longmire & Burge were paid quite significant sums in 1872 and 1874. One of these might relate to the dismantling of the main north-facing studio window, originally of stone, which was rebuilt in cast iron, to maximise the flow of light. (Alternatively this work might have been undertaken at the same time as the extension to the studio: it had certainly been completed by 1880.) The reason for this relative lull was that plans were finally afoot for the major extension to the west of the house that was always intended. The form it would take, however, had surely never been in Leighton's mind when he and Aitchison first conceived the house.

In late 1857, Leighton had travelled to Algiers. He later wrote, 'this visit made a deep impression on me; I have loved "The East" as it is called, ever since.' A decade later, he sailed down the Danube from Vienna into the Black Sea and then on to Turkey, stopping first in Constantinople (Istanbul) and then Broussa (Bursa) and Smyrna (Izmir) before going on by sea to Rhodes, where he certainly collected examples of Lindos-ware pottery. The following year he was in Egypt travelling on the Nile, and in August 1869, he met the diplomat, explorer and linguist Richard Burton at Vichy in France. Burton was on the point of departing for Damascus as British Consul. Leighton appears to have asked him to look out for ceramic tiles and artefacts for his growing collection. Burton took up the commission with gusto, writing to Leighton in March 1871:

> I am quite as willing to have a house pulled down for you now as when at Vichy, but the difficulty is to find a house with tiles. The *bric-a-brac* sellers have quite learned their value.

However, this source was about to dry up. Burton was effectively dismissed from his post in August 1871 and returned to London. The following spring Leighton began working on his celebrated portrait of Burton, exhibited at the Royal Academy in 1876. Burton's departure perhaps prompted Leighton to travel to Damascus himself in October 1873. His main contact was Burton's friend, the Rev. Dr William Wright, an Irish Presbyterian missionary and amateur archaeologist. Wright had been in the city since about 1865: he knew Damascus intimately, spoke fluent Arabic and immediately took Leighton under his wing. 'One of our recreations', as he put it, 'was searching for oriental draperies, and we had many rich finds.' But their principal interest was in 'tiles and plates and long-necked jars with

blue ground and white flowers and during the spare hours of a few weeks, Leighton was able to lay the foundations of his fine collection'.

We cannot be certain when Leighton determined to build his own Arab Hall. Perhaps it was as a result of discussions with Burton at Vichy and was already being planned by the time he set off for Damascus; or maybe the idea came to him after seeing the mosques and 'beautiful old houses' in the city. Within a few years of his return, however, he possessed such a quantity of tiles, that the only conceivable means of displaying them was to build an extension. Wright had become a good friend and continued to supply material from Damascus, the source of the vast majority of

the tiles in the Arab Hall. In January 1874 he was paid £42; a further £46 followed in June 1875. Wright ultimately gave his own collection to Leighton.

Burton meanwhile, had been posted to Trieste in 1872. As a young man, he had served in the army in India and in late 1875 he set off to retrace his steps on a journey recorded in *Sindh Revisited*, published in 1877. Earlier in the year, further sittings for his portrait had taken him back to Leighton's studio, giving Leighton a chance to reiterate his interest in acquiring more tiles. Burton travelled to sites on the banks of the Indus river and made 'a small collection of select fragments' for his 'artistic friend'. On his return to Trieste in July 1876 he wrote to Leighton:

> One word to say that the tiles are packed, and will be sent by the first London steamer – opportunities are rare here. Some are perfect, many are broken; but they will make a bit of mosaic after a little trimming, and illustrate the difference between the Syriac and Sindi. They are taken from the tomb (Moslem) of Sakhar, on the Indus. I can give you analysis of the glaze if you want it; but I fancy you don't care for analyses. The yellow colour is by far the rarest and least durable apparently. The blues are the favourites and the best.

The final parts of this substantial jigsaw came via yet another source, Caspar Purdon

Clarke. Clarke, who would ultimately become Director of the South Kensington Museum (now the Victoria & Albert Museum) and, from 1905, of the Metropolitan Museum in New York, had studied architecture at the National Art Training School at South Kensington. In 1874 he was responsible for constructing Government buildings in Tehran and surveying consular property in Persia. Two years later, he was commissioned by South Kensington to travel to Greece, Turkey and Syria to collect 'art objects' for the museum.

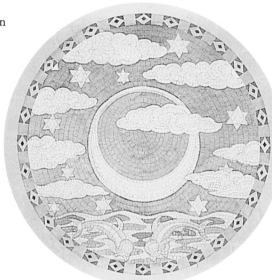

> Before I started Leighton asked me, if I went to Damascus to go to certain houses and try to effect the purchase of certain tiles. I had no difficulty in finding my market, for Leighton, with his customary precision, had accurately indicated every point about the dwellings concerned, and their treasures. I returned with a precious load, and in it some large family tiles, the two finest of which are built into the sides of the alcove of the Arab Hall. Leighton made no difficulty about the price, and insisted on paying double what I had given. He never spoke of picking things up cheap, and scouted the idea of 'bargains' in Art objects.

Leighton's accounts in fact include one payment to Clarke of just £20 in August 1877. His precision about where the desired

tiles were to be found may have stemmed from photographs of buildings and parts of the city that interested him, commissioned when he was in Damascus in 1873. He also had his own sketches and notes to refer to. A third possibility was that William Wright, who retired to London in 1876, was able to provide up-to-date information which was passed on to Clarke.

With Clarke's contributions, the collection consisted of some 1000 individual tiles, mostly from Damascus, as well as plates, vases, textiles and coloured glass windows. By this stage, Aitchison and Leighton were already well advanced with the designs for the Arab Hall. In July 1877, Aitchison produced a section drawing showing how the proposed double-height space would be linked to the existing house by a connecting corridor – now known as the Narcissus Hall. Above the corridor was a room lit by a large domed roof-light. The decorative treatment of the Arab Hall is schematically illustrated but the basic form of the extension changed little through to completion.

In the autumn Leighton travelled to Spain and Tangiers, and in December 1877 the first payment was made to the building contractor, J. Woodward of Finsbury Park. The main structure was largely complete by the middle of 1879; the installation of the marble cladding and columns followed. The specialist plasterwork, painted decoration, gilding and installation of the tiles and mosaic floors continued on through 1880.

19 *Perspective drawing of the house and new Arab Hall from the north west, Building News, 1880.*

20 *Aitchison's design for the Arab Hall extension, July 1877.*

By early October, when the house was again written up in the *Building News*, the Arab Hall is described as finished, although the gold mosaic frieze designed by Walter Crane was probably not finally completed until 1881 or even 1882. Tiles were still being hung in the adjoining Narcissus Hall and the mosaic floors in the original staircase hall were also probably not completed until well into 1881.

Also added in this phase of building was a small library on the ground floor. Leighton would use its flat roof as a terrace accessed from a door opposite his bedroom. The position of the front door was changed, now that the idea of a symmetrical façade had been abandoned, and the breakfast room was also altered to form a new entrance hall, improving the reception of visitors.

The whole project had been a vastly expensive enterprise. Woodward & Co. alone were paid just over £3,000; the total cost including Aitchison's fees was approximately £7,000, comfortably more than had been spent on the entire house up to that date. It is striking how little additional 'useful' accommodation was provided for this sum. There was the new library, but the house remained with just a single bedroom. The majority of the space and resources went into the creation of the Arab Hall, whose purpose was primarily to display the tiles: 'a little addition for the sake of something beautiful to look at once in a while', as Leighton phlegmatically put it. After the first phase of building in 1866, it remained possible for the house to evolve, in terms of accommodation, into a conventional family home. The completion of the Arab Hall extension signalled that this was not going to happen, confirming Leighton's bachelor status and emphasising that aesthetic considerations were now for him paramount.

21 *The north façade of the house showing the completed winter studio, c.1895.*

22 *Detail of Aitchison's presentation drawing of the Silk Room, April 1895.*

23 *Plans of the house as it stood in 1896, based on those in La Constuction Moderne. For the basement see pl.96.*

24 *The south elevation of the house in 1896. A comparison with pl.11 demonstrates how it had evolved over the previous thirty years. From La Constuction Moderne.*

Through the mid 1880s, payments continued to be made to Aitchison: these may relate to redecoration works in the staircase hall during this period. At the end of the decade, attention again turned to improving the studio facilities.

The Winter Studio: 1889–90

For any artist working in London, the poor natural light through the winter months, made worse by the regular impenetrable fogs and smogs, was a significant problem. While for many, including Leighton, it was the excuse for prolonged trips to warmer and brighter climates, it also compressed the time available to work on Academy submissions. In addition, Leighton had worried about his eyesight from his earliest days in Rome. One interviewer elicited from him the fact that he always painted wearing bi-focal glasses: the continued deterioration of his eyesight meant that maximising available daylight became increasingly important. Marcus Stone's studio-house, built in 1875 directly across the back of the garden from Leighton's, had a glass studio built onto the side of the main studio from the start. Leighton would have had plenty of opportunities to admire it from afar.

Aitchison's plan and elevations for the winter studio are dated June 1889 and show what was effectively a glass house supported on cast iron columns. It butted up against the east end of the studio with the existing large window knocked through to form a doorway. The north and east walls were glazed, with the south wall overlooking the street built in brick. In October 1889 work was underway, Leighton commenting in a letter written from Pisa that the studio was 'very tricky and everything more or less inaccessible as I have workmen in the house'. By the following February, the artist Luke Fildes, his neighbour in Melbury Road, noted:

> Leighton, at last, has got into his glass-house but I have not seen him since – I have some interest in the subject as it was I who induced him to build one – I understand his contract was £1,600 for it. Pretty stiff! But that's because of Aitchison who has made a base for it sufficient to support the Eiffel Tower.

Leighton's accounts do not suggest a cost of this order for the works. The glass structure was partly built by Thos Helliwell, a patent glazing contractor, horticultural builder and zinc roofing manufacturer of 9 Victoria Street, at a cost of £135.

Following the completion of the winter studio came another brief lull before work started on the final extension, scarcely completed before Leighton's death.

The Silk Room: 1894–5

Throughout the development of the house, Leighton had been acquiring objects and paintings. These included a significant collection of work presented by his contemporaries or purchased by him to give

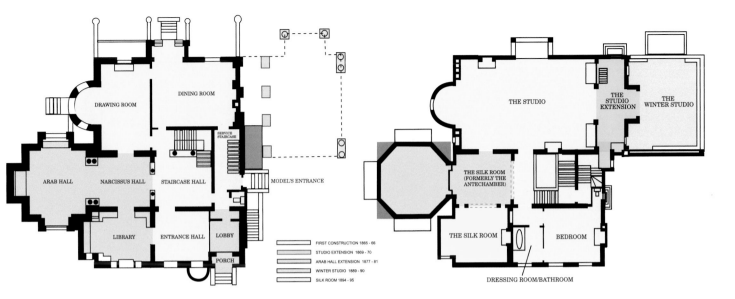

FIRST CONSTRUCTION 1865 - 66
STUDIO EXTENSION 1869 - 70
ARAB HALL EXTENSION 1877 - 81
WINTER STUDIO 1889 - 90
SILK ROOM 1894 - 95

support. By the 1890s, he needed additional hanging space and the idea of building on top of the library was conceived. This meant that Leighton lost his roof terrace, but with ever more building up and down Holland Park Road, it had become an increasingly public retreat. The new gallery was a simple space, without windows and lit by a single large domed rooflight.

As with all the previous phases of construction, a new firm of builders was appointed to carry out the work. Patman & Fotheringham of Theobald's Road started work in the second half of 1894 and the new gallery was sufficiently complete to be open for Leighton's annual (and final) musical gathering in March of the following year. In April 1895, Aitchison produced a section through the new gallery showing it furnished and complete – the only anomaly is that the dolphin frieze circling the room is picked out in colour, though there is no evidence that this was ever carried out. It is possible that Leighton's deteriorating health through 1895, and his long absences abroad during the year, meant that completion was dragged out and the new room

never entirely finished. Certainly Patman & Fotheringham are amongst Leighton's creditors after his death, 'for balance of contract for new picture gallery & repairs'.

At around this date, the house was converted to electricity, supplied by the Notting Hill Electric Light Company, and with the completion of the Silk Room, what had started as a relatively modest house thirty years earlier was now an extraordinary architectural statement that reflected both Leighton's financial and professional standing and Aitchison's confidence and experience. The interiors formed a series

of carefully composed and interconnected spaces along two key axes. The first encompassed the transition from staircase hall to Narcissus Hall to Arab Hall on the ground floor. The second was the move from dark to light as the stairs were climbed, and the grandeur of the painting studio reached on the first floor. The ensemble continued to resist any easy stylistic categorisation, reflecting Leighton's catholic tastes. 'His mind', wrote Joseph Hatton in 1883, 'is large enough to take in the eclecticism of Greek art, the devotionalism of the Mediaeval and the warmth of Orientalism.'

Fig. 6. — Façade méridionale.

From House to Museum

25 Opposite: Detail of marquetry and ivory inlay in one of the doors of the cabinet returned to the studio in 2011.

26 Leighton's will, leaving his entire estate to his sisters Augusta and Alexandra.

27 An embroidered Turkish 'Qibleh' cloth, usually hung in a tent to indicate the direction of prayer facing Mecca, acquired by Glasgow Museums in 1896, following the sale.

28 An Iznik dish, c.1565, that may have formed part of Leighton's collections. He certainly owned similar examples.

Leighton died on 25 January 1896. His brief handwritten will, drawn up only shortly beforehand, left 'the whole estate unconditionally' to his two sisters, Alexandra Orr and Augusta Matthews. They had been at his bedside for the previous two days and between attacks of angina he had made them aware of his last wishes. Also present in these final hours were Leighton's neighbour Val Prinsep and the artist Samuel Pepys Cockerell. Dorothy Dene, his principal model and muse for the last years of his life was admitted to say her farewell. Leighton's last words reflected his careful separation of public and private personae to the end. 'My love to the Academy', a phrase that was widely reported in the obituaries, was not in fact his final utterance. This was in German, 'for his sisters' ears alone'. Leighton wished to settle substantial sums on certain individuals and make a large bequest to the Royal Academy. He apparently indicated that he was content for the house to be sold to achieve the required funds. Leighton's sisters offered the house and all its contents for £25,000 in the hope that funds could be raised to establish it as a museum in their brother's memory. Support was not forthcoming and they made plans for the sale of the house alone. A brochure was drawn up for auction of the house on 19 May 1896, but it failed to attract a sufficient bid: with only one bedroom it was 'too far restricted for a family' and it was 'bought in' at £12,000. Attention then turned instead to the sale of the contents.

The Sale of Leighton's Collections

From Wednesday 8 July through to 16 July 1896, Leighton's entire collection was sold at the King Street premises of Christie, Manson & Woods. (Not included were his own studies and sketchbooks. Numbering approximately 1600 examples in total, these drawings were sold to the Fine Art Society: many would return to the house in the years immediately following, see p.77.) A summary of the Christie's sale catalogues indicates the quantity and variety of the collections, gathered over a lifetime.

The first three days were devoted to decorative art material, the biggest single

29 *Pasture, Egypt, 1868, one of the many landscape sketches by Leighton included in the sale.*

30 *Wind on the Wold, 1863, by George Hemming Mason (1818–72), one of several artists generously supported by Leighton. Eight works by him were in the sale: this example was purchased by Sir Henry Tate and presented by him to the Tate Gallery.*

group being 82 examples of 'Rhodian, Anatolian and Persian pottery'. This reflected Leighton's strong personal taste for middle-eastern artefacts, though 24 lots of 'Chinese enamelled and blue and white porcelain' and 28 of 'Satsuma and other Japanese pottery' represented the oriental collecting that had been so fashionable in artistic circles in the 1870s. English porcelain numbered just 7 lots although one of these was Leighton's 107-piece Lowestoft dinner service bearing his coat of arms.

Carpets and textiles consisted of 48 'Old Persian prayer rugs, carpets etc.' and 63 lots of 'Costumes, Oriental and European embroideries and brocades'. Two six-fold Japanese screens, a Turkish scimitar and a Moorish casket were among 39 lots of 'Oriental objects of art'. Miscellaneous items used as props, including a crossbow and a mandolin, together with fixtures and fittings familiar from photographs – the stuffed peacock and copper cistern from the staircase hall – together amounted to 40 lots.

Furniture was catalogued under three headings. 'Old Italian and other decorative furniture', 18 lots; 'English furniture' a further 17 lots including the three bookcases and enormous sideboard designed by Aitchison for the house; and 'Decorative furniture', 13 lots including the armchairs inlaid with mirror and ivory from either side of the dining-room fireplace. Altogether 55 chairs were sold.

The sale of the paintings began on 11 July with Leighton's own landscape studies in oil. These had lined the walls of the studio and recorded his innumerable travels: 212 were sold in total, together with a further 35 studies for exhibited pictures and a limited number of finished works. Then followed Leighton's collection of works on paper by other artists, including his contemporaries Edward Burne-Jones, Albert Moore, G.F. Watts and Simeon Solomon, as well as by Ingres, Delacroix and Thomas Gainsborough. The paintings collection totalled a further 63 lots: Leighton's friends and contemporaries featured strongly, with George Hemming Mason and Giovanni Costa, artist friends who received generous financial support from him over many years, particularly well represented. Works by the French landscape painters Leighton

31 *Lord Rockingham and Edmund Burke (unfinished), by Sir Joshua Reynolds (1723–92), the first President of the Royal Academy. Leighton acquired the painting in 1879 from the collection of his predecessor as President, Sir Francis Grant.*

32 *A study of David and Goliath by Michelangelo Buonarroti (1475–1564). Four studies of this subject were originally on a single sheet in Leighton's collection. Michelangelo was a source of deep inspiration to him. 'When you put your hand on this drawing,' he commented, 'you touch the hand of the master.'*

31 *Lord Rockingham and Edmund Burke (unfinished), by Sir Joshua Reynolds (1723–92), the first President of the Royal Academy. Leighton acquired the painting in 1879 from the collection of his predecessor as President, Sir Francis Grant.*

32 *A study of David and Goliath by Michelangelo Buonarroti (1475–1564). Four studies of this subject were originally on a single sheet in Leighton's collection. Michelangelo was a source of deep inspiration to him. 'When you put your hand on this drawing,' he commented, 'you touch the hand of the master.'*

so admired, including Jean-Baptiste-Camille Corot, Charles-Francois Daubigny and Eugène Fromentin, also made a strong group. Further artists represented were John Constable (four works), David Cox, Joshua Reynolds and Leighton's predecessor as President of the Royal Academy, Sir Francis Grant. The Old Master collection numbered 31 lots, including numerous paintings attributed to Venetian artists of the sixteenth century – Jacopo Bassano, Paris Bordone, Andrea Schiavone, Sebastiano del Piombo and Jacopo Tintoretto.

The sale ended on 15 and 16 July with Leighton's library, his artist's proofs of engravings made from his works, his collections of Japanese prints and Old Master etchings, engravings and drawings, including examples by Michelangelo and Leonardo da Vinci. The library itself consisted of over 300 titles covering architectural history, biography, philosophy and history in several languages.

The circumstances of the sale had virtually assured its success. Bidders included several of the established London dealers. Agnew & Sons and Colnaghi, both of whom had dealt in Leighton's works over many years were particularly prominent. Amongst fellow artists who secured souvenirs were Val Prinsep, Lawrence Alma-Tadema, Edward Poynter and Charles Fairfax Murray. George Aitchison bought one of the bookcases he had designed together with the plaster cast of Leighton's sculpture *Needless Alarms*.

In August 1896 the sisters received the proceeds of the sale: £31,549 9s 1d. They were able immediately to discharge their brother's wishes, giving £10,000 to the Royal Academy, £5,000 to Dorothy Dene, and a further £5,000 to the Dene Trust established to support Dorothy's siblings, three of whom had also modelled for Leighton. £3,000 was given to his great friend, Giovanni Costa. The residue of the estate was paid into an account to be administered jointly by Alexandra and Augusta.

The Fate of the House

The house no longer needed to be sold and the question of what to do with it began to preoccupy the sisters. At the forefront of discussions was Emilie Barrington (pl.33), Leighton's near neighbour in Melbury Road, who had become increasingly involved in the lives of the Holland Park Circle, and who would write the first major biography of Leighton, published in 1906. Mrs Barrington was the driving force behind the formation of the Leighton House Committee in 1897, chaired by Sir Lionel Cust, Director of the National Portrait Gallery, with the object of saving the house for the nation. With the blessing of the Prince of Wales it gathered an impressive list of supporters including the Archbishops of Canterbury and York, several noblemen, the Lord Chief Justice and other prominent society figures. The actor Sir Henry Irving and the artists G.F. Watts, Hamo Thornycroft, William Blake Richmond and George Frampton lent their names to the cause, while George Aitchison, Caspar Purdon Clarke and William De Morgan represented those who had been involved in the creation of the house.

In April 1898 Leighton's sisters assigned the leases on the property and

the committee became tenants. Initially the house could be viewed by appointment through Mrs Barrington and it was not until April 1900 that it formally opened to the public. The committee established a programme of lectures and concerts and started to form a permanent collection (see p.77) while raising an endowment to maintain and operate the new museum.

There were evidently personality clashes, and not all Leighton's friends were supportive. In 1900, affronted by the committee's proposal that Holland Park Road should be renamed Leighton House Street, Val Prinsep wrote to the Clerk of the Kensington Vestry that such a move was 'not for the honour of the late Lord Leighton, but to aid the schemes of those who wish to "exploit" his memory for their personal glorification'. Prinsep had been at the house when Leighton died and felt that at no time had his friend indicated any interest in being commemorated as was now being proposed. Leighton's sisters responded in wounded fashion that no one should claim to know their brother's wishes better than they, and that 'two old and broken women' felt betrayed by the attitude of their brother's erstwhile friend.

The financial situation of the Committee remained uncertain, as it had proved difficult to interest 'men of wealth' sufficiently to secure an endowment. In 1901, a permanent solution appeared to have been found. The committee approached the newly established Municipal Borough of Kensington to 'signalise their inaugural year of office by acquiring the House': this was unanimously passed and detailed discussions for the transfer began. But at the eleventh hour, Mrs Barrington intervened. Despite having been present at all negotiations, she now stated her complete opposition to the sale: a letter was sent by her husband to the sisters stating that 'I cannot see any guarantee, or even probability, that the House and its contents, which you and I prize so dearly, would be maintained in a manner worthy of the dignity of its associations'. Alexandra wrote immediately to the Committee that 'the present negotiations with the Kensington Borough Council cannot proceed without discredit to our brother's memory if they fail, and a probably deeper injury to it if they are successful'. She and Augusta would rather the house were destroyed or sold to a private individual than that it become a venue for unnamed parish 'business'. Faced with this opposition, the frustrated Committee wound itself up, and handed back the tenancy. Perhaps Mrs Barrington was acting in the best interests of the house, although it is also clear that she knew her personal influence could not

be guaranteed following a transfer.

Responsibility for Leighton House then fell to Mrs Barrington and a small group of supporters. In 1908, serious consideration was given to the odd idea of re-erecting the fifteenth-century Crosby Hall, dismantled from its original location in Bishopsgate, in the garden.

In 1910–11 the London County Council was approached to take over the house, but declined on the grounds of its unsuitability for use as 'an important public institution'. Two years later discussions were held with the Imperial Arts League but again these came to nothing. By the 1920s, both Leighton's sisters were dead and

the need for a long-term solution became more pressing. In 1925, the Leighton House Association, formed by Emilie Barrington as a successor to the Leighton House Committee was wound up and after a protracted process, the Council finally purchased the freehold from the Ilchester Estate for £2,750. To gain a public entertainments licence, immediate works were required to improve the heating (hitherto provided by open fires) and to introduce an external fire-escape from the winter studio.

In February 1927, Mrs Ida Perrin, who lived locally in Holland Villas Road, approached the Council offering to pay for a new extension to provide additional

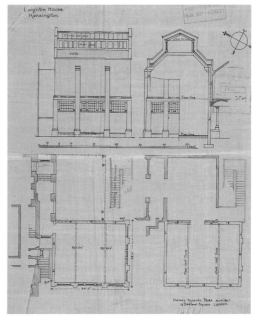

gallery space. She engaged the architect Halsey Ricardo, the designer of nearby Debenham House in Addison Road, to draw up a scheme for a two storey extension to the south of the winter studio containing a single large gallery space on each floor. The scheme was broadly accepted in May 1927 and the Council approached the Ilchester Estate for its approval. The estate agreed on the ground that the new building would advantageously obscure the iron structure of Leighton's winter studio! Halsey Ricardo died in February 1928 and the project was completed by Henry Fletcher, and opened by Princess Louise in May 1929.

Linking the new Perrin extension to the east end of the house was achieved at some cost to the original fabric. The model's entrance was obscured, the loggia internalised and a new door knocked through into the dining room. Internally, the original decorative schemes were also being eroded. There is no record of any alterations made prior to the transfer of the building to the Council. However, extensive internal redecoration was carried out in the 1930s when the house was a venue for general cultural activities, with concerts in the studio remaining popular. To maximise seating

capacity, the large screen that stood at the east of the room was taken down in 1935.

In 1940 and again in 1944 the house was badly damaged by wartime bombs, although by good fortune the impact was at the opposite end of the house to the Arab Hall. The second explosion blew out glass in much of the house and caused 'roof damage serious enough to endanger the contents through rain'. The house was boarded up but clearly there was significant damp penetration. Competing post-war priorities meant that damaged roofs and windows had to wait until 1947 for repair, and it was not until 1950–1 that extensive restoration works were completed. The house remained closed to the public throughout this 11-year period. Whatever might have remained of the original decorative schemes was almost certainly lost in the drive to get the house serviceable again. New heating and lighting systems were introduced, and with limited funds available no attempt was made to recreate the appearance of the house as Leighton had left it. Fluorescent tube lighting was hung from the ceilings and the walls were painted cream.

The period through the 1950s and into the 1960s saw the appreciation of

Victorian art and architecture at its lowest ebb. With the intention of finding a new use for the building, the Borough's Junior Library was relocated to the ground floor of the Perrin extension in 1952. The house remained in demand as a concert venue. Lectures were regularly held in the studio, although Leighton and his contemporaries were largely ignored as potential subjects. Exhibitions were almost all of contemporary artists. The house also became a meeting place for groups such as the Kensington Lodge of the Philosophical Society. In 1955, the Council installed new toilet and kitchen facilities beneath Leighton's winter studio. Poorly designed and cheaply constructed, these works again had a detrimental impact on the original fabric, completely obscuring the east elevation.

In 1961, a nadir was reached. G.F. Watts' studio-house in Melbury Road was demolished and flats built on the site. While it was not immediately threatened, Leighton House's future was not secure. Attempts by the London County Council to have a preservation order imposed on the house and the other artists' houses nearby were resisted by the Council, leading to a public enquiry and letters to the press expressing

39 *The mosaic floors being surveyed prior to the start of the major refurbishment of 2009–10.*

40 *The restoration of the dome of the Arab Hall in 2009–10. The painted decoration was applied first and then gilded around with great care.*

41 *Gilding the Arab Hall dome.*

fears that Leighton House might be lost.

Only at the very end of the decade did the outlook begin to change. On 17 December 1969 the constituent meeting of the Friends of Leighton House was held. With Sir John Betjeman as President, the Chairman was John Yeoman and Vice-Chairman Betjeman's daughter Candida Lycett Green. The Friends began to promote the house and bring influential people to support its restoration and the development of the permanent collections. The first retrospective exhibitions devoted to Leighton's contemporaries began to be held. Books and articles re-evaluated their work and in 1975, Richard and Leonée Ormond published their seminal book on Leighton.

Finally, in 1982, Stephen Jones was appointed curator of Leighton House. By this date, no original decorative finish, with the exception of the tiles, remained. With great energy he embarked on the long process of recreating the original appearance of the interiors, based on photographic evidence, paint analysis and contemporary descriptions. The Royal Borough of Kensington and Chelsea invested substantial sums in repairs to the basic fabric and strong support from the Friends of Leighton House, bolstered by sponsorship from individuals and companies, allowed each room to be slowly recreated. This work was continued under Stephen Jones' successors, Joanna Banham (1989–92) and Julia Findlater (1992–8).

The major programme of refurbishment and restoration undertaken through 2009 was prompted by a condition survey of the building completed three years earlier. This had identified the need to re-wire the building, replace the ageing fire and intruder alarms and upgrade the central heating system. From these beginnings, a comprehensive project evolved addressing many other aspects of the building and encompassing the complete redecoration of the interiors. In the following room by room descriptions, information is provided about how each interior was decorated and furnished in Leighton's day and how their original appearance has now been recreated.

The Interiors

42 *The Arab Hall.*

43 *The house from Holland Park Road in the early twentieth century.*

44 *Icarus, commissioned by Leighton in 1882 from the sculptor Alfred Gilbert (1854–1934).*

Leighton claimed that he lived 'in a mews': certainly the exterior of the house did little to indicate the splendours inside. Opposite were nondescript cottages and stables, and the unremarkable entrance façade was itself screened by a row of plane and lime trees planted along the boundary wall.

The Entrance Hall

Internally, the reception areas were altered substantially in Leighton's lifetime. The front door was originally on axis with the door into the garden from the dining room on the north side of the building. Immediately inside was a small lobby leading directly to the staircase hall (pl.12).

Leighton's breakfast room, occupying much of what is now the entrance hall, was a simple rectangular room with two windows overlooking the street, entered from the staircase hall. There was a fireplace at its east end, adjacent to where the front door is now located. Visitors calling on any kind

of business had therefore to be let into the staircase hall at the heart of the house. As their number grew, the creation of a reception room where visitors could be asked to wait or where Leighton could receive certain callers without admitting them to the more private parts of the house became pressing.

As part of the major works of 1877–81, the front door was moved to its current position and the wall between the original lobby and the breakfast room was taken down. A new lobby, separated from the rest of the space by a glazed screen, had its own access into the back staircase to allow for the servants' prompt attendance at the front door (pl.23).

To heighten a sense of anticipation and in keeping with its functional nature, the new entrance hall was plainly decorated in 'a calm tone – stone colour walls hung with a few drawings'. One of these, a view of the *Fontana della Tartarughe* in Rome, was by Leighton's inspirational painting master, Edward von Steinle. A large plaster picture frame 2.5m high containing a canvas attributed to 'the Venetian school' was cemented into the north wall, the companion to the painting that remains in the adjacent library. The frame was removed in 1988. In the doorway through to the library stood *Icarus* by the sculptor Alfred Gilbert. In 1882 Leighton called on Gilbert, who was staying near Perugia with his family, and offered him £100 to produce a statuette of any style and subject. The result was *Icarus*, exhibited at the Royal Academy in 1884

and now in the collections of the National Museum of Wales, Cardiff. For his part, Gilbert, in remarks made in Leighton's studio shortly after his death commented, 'all I know, and all the little I have been able to do as a sculptor, I owe to Leighton'.

The Staircase Hall

It was George Aitchison's opinion that 'well designed staircases are perhaps the most striking features in mansions or public buildings'. When first built, the scale and grandeur of the staircase hall anticipated later additions, but it also recognised the importance of the staircase as the almost ceremonial route taking visitors and

45 A drawing of the staircase hall, Building News 1876, looking towards the dining room, showing the original tiled floor in situ. Leighton's cast of Narcissus is on the left.

46 The courtyard of the fifteenth-century Palazzo Centani, Venice.

47 View of the staircase hall, 1895.

prospective buyers up to the studio on the first floor. The impact must have been even greater when the building was first completed and the visitor entered via a small lobby leading from the front door. Aitchison and Leighton seem to have invested more in this opportunity to impress than in the principal reception rooms beyond. Over subsequent years the staircase hall continued to demand attention. Its decoration went through more changes than any other part of the house.

A key influence on Leighton as he planned his home was the architecture and interiors of Venice; Aitchison had also visited the city. It was in the design of the staircase hall that this was felt most keenly. Venetian palazzi prior to the sixteenth century did not often contain internal stair-cases, but to maximise space incorporated them into small courtyards at the rear. A well-head was usually placed at the centre of the space with the stairs running around two sides of the enclosing walls. Leighton's staircase hall clearly refers to this model, most closely resembling the picturesque courtyard of the fifteenth-century Palazzo Centani. The distinctive carved wooden beams supported by stone columns are

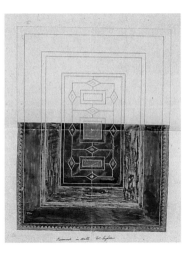

48 *Aitchison's design for the original tiled 'pavement' in the staircase hall, November 1865.*

49 *Iznik blue and turquoise tile dating from the seventeenth century.*

50 *Stencilled decoration from the staircase soffit.*

51 *Detail of embroidery on the staircase seat by Gertrude Jekyll.*

are late fifteenth-century from Damascus and were added later. The inscription, in jumbled Arabic, reads:

> This house has obtained cheerfulness and earnest joy for the helpers, written in good fortune on its doors, enter it with peace, being safe.

features unique to Venetian courtyards of this type. Leighton even placed a large copper urn containing a palm in place of the well-head, its position marked out by the square placed centrally in the mosaic floor.

The Venetian theme was carried through in the sumptuous decoration. The floor was tiled to Aitchison's geometric design. The beams above the stone capitals were painted blue, with the decorative incisions originally in silver. The walls of the upper staircase were painted in an Indian red similar to the main studio, and the staircase itself was varnished pitch pine with an oak stringer. The black painted

door surrounds enriched with incised and gilded decoration, one of the most distinctive features of the house, were introduced from the start, but the same treatment was not applied to the staircase until some twenty years later in the mid 1880s.

The tiles lining the initial flight of the staircase were the first to be installed in the house. Those below the picture rail are Iznik, dating from the early seventeenth century, probably collected on Leighton's expedition to Turkey in 1867. There are tiles very similar to those featuring the blue vase and floral sprays in the Topkapi Palace in Constantinople. The tiles above the rail

The success of this first integration of tiles into the fabric of the building may have planted the seed that would culminate in the construction of the Arab Hall. A second trophy from this Turkish trip was probably the inlaid marriage chest, converted to form a seat on the staircase. The seat cushion was originally embroidered by Gertrude Jekyll (1843–1932). Although best known as a highly influential garden designer, Gertrude Jekyll's early ambition to become a painter was thwarted only by acute myopia. In 1870 having abandoned hopes of a painting career, she began to produce embroidery. Leighton saw her work exhibited at the

London International Exhibition Society in New Bond Street in the same year, describing it as 'of remarkable merit in point of colour and arrangement'. A friendship developed and he commissioned first a tablecloth for his dining table and then the seat on the staircase with two bands of linked floral motifs embroidered on silk. Two of these panels were uncovered in the 1980s and removed for safekeeping (pl.51). In the 2009–10 restoration, they were painstakingly copied and the full set reinstated.

The extension of the house in 1877–81 with the Arab Hall prompted the wholesale revision of the original decorative scheme as Leighton and Aitchison sought to integrate the old and new spaces. The two stone columns between the staircase hall and the Narcissus Hall beyond mark the line of the original external wall which was taken down. Once the new extension was completed, the tiled floor of the staircase hall was taken up and mosaic floors designed by Aitchison and made by Burke & Co. were laid throughout. The peacock blue tiles made by William De Morgan to line the walls of the adjacent Narcissus Hall were carried through into the staircase hall, covering the south and east walls and further blurring the boundaries of old and new.

At about the same time in the early

52 *The staircase hall.*

53 *An illustration of the dining room,* Building News *1876. Aitchison's enormous sideboard can be seen on the right.*

54 *The dining room.*

1880s the soffit of the staircase was decorated in a stencilled gold scheme; the staircase itself was painted black in about 1885. The incised decoration on the blue beams was also changed from silver to gold leaf. The colour of the upper wall surfaces had gone through numerous variations before culminating in a strong ochre. These changes streamlined the decoration in this part of the house into a palette of black, gold and peacock blue. Further integration came from the subtle transfer of motifs from the door surrounds to the mosaic floors and the incised decoration on the staircase itself.

This decorative scheme was gradually lost during the first half of the twentieth century. The 'peculiar blue' of the timber beams was painted over in black, the gilded decoration replaced by gold paint and the soffit of the staircase papered over and painted in gold. The original wall colour was lost beneath redecoration. The staircase hall was first restored in 1984, with further work completed in 1997. Following research by the Architectural Paint Research Unit of English Heritage, the staircase soffit was revealed and restored and in 1999 the whole hall was redecorated. The 2009 restoration changed the upper wall colour from a saffron yellow to a tawny brown. This change followed the discovery of photographs that suggested the saffron scheme, previously thought to date from Leighton's occupation, was in fact introduced in the years immediately following his death.

The Dining Room

Above the door to the dining room in gilded letters is the German word *Prosit* – 'Good health' or 'Cheers'. Leighton was deemed an excellent host and entertained regularly. The dining table could be extended to seat over twenty guests. According to Alice Corkran, it was Leighton's habit 'to sit a little higher than his guests, on a seat from which he could dominate the table'.

At the east end of the room is the large oak fireplace designed by Aitchison and decorated with incised motifs familiar from elsewhere in the house. The two niches either side contained what appear to be rare examples of 'Lamu' chairs made on the east coast of Africa from the seventeenth century. Leighton's were noteworthy for the panels of mirror set into the backs: it is possible that this was a later modification. Above the fireplace hung a painting of *Venus and Cupid* attributed to Andrea Schiavone (untraced) and only two other paintings are recorded hanging in this room, a *Vulcan and Iris* by Paris Bordone (Museum of Art and Archaeology, University of Missouri-Columbia, USA) and *Paul the Hermit* attributed to Jacopo Bassano (untraced). The rest of the interior was given over to the

display of about fifty ceramic plates. Those on display now are replicas produced by Ismail Yigit in Kutahya, Turkey. They have been hung to conform to Leighton's original display.

To the right of the fireplace is the door leading to the servants' staircase and the kitchens in the basement. Occupying the full length of the wall between the doors on this side of the room was a vast ebonised sideboard, over 2.5m long and 2.4m high. Designed by Aitchison, it was inlaid in ivory and light wood with bosses in lapis lazuli. Mrs Haweis in her description of the house published in 1882 wrote that its blackness was broken by 'a crowd of china on its shelves, blue Nankeen and old English and by a pretty little silver coffee service of Turkish work'.

In the centre of the room is Leighton's original dining table, one of the few pieces of his own furniture in the house. In 1870 he asked Gertrude Jekyll to embroider a cloth for it, to be executed in serge and wool or wool and silk and of 'some good design and rich tone'. She produced a design of 'four figures of pots whose flowers converge towards the centre' on a red background. Now untraced, a plain red cloth has been introduced in its place. The dining chairs are not Leighton's but are in oak with brown leather upholstery.

The 1980's restoration uncovered slivers of what was thought to be Leighton's original flock wallpaper but analysis carried out in 2009 determined that it was in fact manufactured after Leighton's death. Only one photograph of the interior of the dining room is known from his time. Of poor

57 *Detail of the decoration on the drawing room fireplace.*

58 *The view from the library across the Narcissus Hall to the drawing room beyond; a vista created as part of the alterations made to the house in 1877–81.*

quality it required careful interpretation. The pattern was developed from this single image and printed using a traditional flocking method near Blackburn, Lancashire. Contemporary descriptions of this interior referred to the 'dull red' colour of the floor. This was stripped away in the twentieth century, but small traces were discovered under the skirting boards and the colour was reinstated as part of the 2009–10 restoration.

The Drawing Room

With the adjacent dining room, the drawing room is part of the first phase of the house completed in 1866. With the studio on the first floor acting as Leighton's principal reception room, the drawing room may have functioned largely as a withdrawing room for women following dinner in the dining room. The contemporary descriptions noted the 'ash-blue' or 'peacock blue' colour of the floor. As with the adjacent dining room, this original finish was stripped off in the twentieth-century, but traces were clearly visible along the edge of loose floorboards when they were lifted. Samples were analysed, colour-matched and the floors repainted in 2010.

The interior is dominated by the large west-facing bay window. The central sash could be lifted to give access down into the garden, although the outlook and the amount of light coming into the room were compromised by the substantial extension of Val Prinsep's house next door in the early 1890s. Weighted wooden shutters that disappear into the floor are still in use, while over the fireplace there is a mirrored shutter that can be pushed back into the wall cavity to the right. The location of a fireplace beneath a window was repeated in two other places in the house. The flue rises to the left up to a conventional chimney. As part of Leighton's lease agreement, he was permitted, were he to leave the property, to remove any fireplace that could be described as a 'Work of Art' and substitute plainer examples, evidence of the thought and cost that had gone into their creation.

Leighton was a pioneering collector of contemporary French painting in England, after his time in Paris in 1855–8. Some of his most important acquisitions were displayed in this room. On the west wall, either side of the bay window, were the four large panels depicting the times of the day by Jean-Baptiste-Camille Corot. Perhaps for aesthetic reasons of his own, Leighton did not hang them in the conventional sequence. *Evening* and *Noon* were paired to the left of the window, *Night* and *Morning* to the right. Painted by Corot for the studio of his friend the artist Alexandre-Gabriel Decamps in Fontainebleau in about 1858, they were bought by the Parisian art publisher Alfred Cadart in January 1865. Leighton's accounts show a payment of £180 to Cadart in August of the same year. In the centre of the circular ceiling over the bay window was a study by Eugène Delacroix for the ceiling of the Salon de la Paix in the Hôtel de Ville, Paris: *La Paix vient consoler les Hommes*, painted in 1852, was acquired by Leighton in Paris in 1864 following the artist's death. The room was clearly designed from the start to incorporate the Delacroix, and the Corots were probably also part of its original conception. They certainly seemed to fit the available space perfectly, and perhaps the semicircular window bay was conceived to emphasise the passage of the sun, admitting a changing light at different times of the day and in different seasons. Leighton acquired the Corots only shortly before construction started, which perhaps required the modification of Aitchison's

plans, but the display of the collection and the form of the house did fuse together in this way. Elsewhere in the room hung another landscape by Corot, *Evening on the Lake* (now in the National Gallery, London) and a landscape by Charles-François Daubigny. Here too was John Constable's study for his celebrated *The Hay Wain*, one of four Constables owned by Leighton that complemented the *plein air* works of the French artists displayed.

The wallpaper was recreated in the restoration of 1984–5 based on contemporary photographs and descriptions of its colour; 'nut-brown' or that of 'a good cigar' and hand-blocked by Mornay in Paris. The curtains are a lampas fabric in greens, browns and creams and were installed as part of the 2009–10 restoration. A painstaking examination of the original photograph of the interior suggested that lampas would best reproduce the pattern and texture of the curtains shown in place in 1895. The same photograph was used to reintroduce furnishings to the large window bay. In the centre of the room hangs a mid-nineteenth-century Murano glass chandelier. This is not Leighton's own, but is a close match to that shown in place in 1895. A copy of the Delacroix roundel, now in the Musée Carnavalet, Paris, was made in 1987 by Tim Rukavina. Copies of Corot's *The Four Times of the Day* were painted in 2009–10 by Charlie Cobb.

59 *The Narcissus Hall, 1895.*

60 *A Damascus hexagonal tile, c.1570.*

61 *Night, by Jean-Baptiste-Camille Corot (1796–1875). Corot's 'Four Times of the Day' series was amongst Leighton's most treasured possessions. The picture can be seen in pl.55.*

The Narcissus Hall

The Narcissus Hall, constructed as part of the extension of 1877–81, and described in contemporary accounts as a 'corridor', served to connect the original house with the Arab Hall beyond. Aitchison deliberately inserted a compressed space between the larger volumes of the staircase hall at one end and the Arab Hall at the other, heightening the drama of the transition between them. A new set of double doors gave access into the drawing room and,

opposite, matching doors opened into the library also constructed at this time.

At the centre of the room is a bronze cast of *Narcissus* – although not Leighton's own version. The original bronze was excavated and identified as Narcissus at Pompeii in August 1862. As with other Pompeian statuary, it was rapidly commercialised: numerous copies were sold. Leighton had secured his cast before embarking on the extension, and the Narcissus Hall seems to

craft, by the mid 1870s he became increasingly expert in the colours and glazes of Ottoman pottery, often referred to as the 'Persian' style. Leighton invited De Morgan to a breakfast meeting where the Arab Hall project was discussed.

De Morgan was paid a total of £227 for his work between July 1880 and January 1882, although such was his perfectionism, that it was apparently completed at a personal loss of £500 – a fact he felt he could not reveal to Leighton. Filling the space between dado and cornice the tiles possess an exceptional depth of colour achieved only after De Morgan had rejected many 'failures'. The wall surface is articulated by bands of gold mosaic and further enriched by the pairs of hexagonal Iznik tiles dating from about 1530 that are set into it. Above the doors to the drawing room is a panel of nine tiles from Damascus dating from the late sixteenth century, and on the opposite side above the library doors a panel of Iznik tiles of about 1530.

More practical considerations included the provision of central heating, with pipes running beneath the grills on each side of the room and beyond into the Arab Hall.

The original gilded decoration of the ceiling was probably lost as a result of damp penetration in the 1940s. In the post-war restoration the ceiling was repaired and then covered over with lining paper painted in gold paint. In 1999, the lining paper was removed and a match made to the remnants of the original gold leaf. The ceiling was then prepared and gilded.

have been conceived around it. As contemporary commentators noted, the silvery-gold ceiling reflecting the deep blue of the tiles created a watery effect heightened by the rippling light thrown by the gasolier in the centre of the room. The setting evoked the Narcissus legend – a young man falls in love with his own reflection in a pool and unable to tear himself away, pines and dies. A further indication that the sculpture was always intended for this position is the link between the pink marble rectangle in the centre of the room and the red and yellow streaked brocatello plinth Leighton had commissioned for the sculpture. Even the flower motifs in grey mosaic at each corner of the floor can be read as stylised narcissi. Ironically, the sculpture is now thought to represent Dionysus rather than Narcissus, but this subtle interplay of the collection and its setting underlined the cultivated ambience.

The other striking element of the interior is the wonderful tiles made by William De Morgan (1839–1917). After training as a painter at the Royal Academy Schools and then, with the encouragement of his friend William Morris, designing and producing stained glass, William De Morgan became the foremost potter associated with the Arts and Crafts Movement. Fascinated by the technical and scientific aspects of his

64 *The furnished Arab Hall, c.1890.*

65 *The interior of the twelfth-century palace of La Zisa, Palermo, the inspiration for Leighton's Arab Hall. See also pl.42 for comparison.*

The Arab Hall

The Arab Hall was the centrepiece of the extension to the house of 1877–81. The interior is based on a reception room at the Sicilio-Norman palace of La Zisa at Palermo in Sicily, started by William I in 1164 and completed in about 1180 by his son, William II. Constructed for summer use, the palace was surrounded by 'beautiful fruit-bearing trees and pleasant gardens', themselves part of a much larger park. By the nineteenth century, the palace may have lost some of its perfection, but remained a popular destination for visiting architects. William Burges made tracings of the mosaics and sketched details in the early 1850s, and his friend the architect Frederick Pepys Cockerell also made drawings of the palace in the spring of 1857. While there is no record of Aitchison having visited, Leighton travelled in Sicily and was certainly at La Zisa. An undated sketchbook held at the Royal Academy (LEI/6) contains annotated drawings of the capitals in the angles of the walls.

Quite when this interior emerged as the model from which the Arab Hall would be created is not known, but once identified, Aitchison and Leighton were relatively faithful to it. Walter Crane, who designed the gold mosaic frieze around the interior, visited La Zisa 'many years afterwards' and was surprised by 'how closely the plan and proportions of the old palace hall had been followed'. Certain details were almost exactly replicated. For example, the six capitals carved by the celebrated Austrian-born sculptor Edgar Boehm (1834–90) are so close that he must have been working from photographs or detailed drawings of the originals (pls 66, 67). (Boehm does not appear to have been paid, perhaps completing the work as a gift to Leighton.) Aitchison himself must have had access to more photographs if not precise measured drawings as he began work. Itself an amalgam of Byzantine, Arab and Norman influences, La Zisa was a peculiarly appropriate model for the various source materials that Leighton would bring to the

66 *Detail of one of the carved capitals by Edgar Boehm in the Arab Hall.*

67 *Detail of one of the carved capitals at La Zisa.*

68 *A De Morgan tile (the parrot perched on the left of the fountain) made to complete a late sixteenth-century panel from Damascus.*

69 *Detail of the mosaic floor in the Arab Hall.*

creation of his own Arab Hall. Its success derives from the combination of original old tiles, windows and woodwork with the contributions of the contemporary designers and craftsmen assembled to carry out the interior.

The plan, a square with recesses, follows that at La Zisa and is typical of the hall plan of many palaces and mausolea across the Islamic world. The two sets of columns flanking the entrance to the room, the division of the wall surface into three, the gold mosaic frieze, the use of marble cladding and the inclusion of a pool at the centre of the room are all taken more or less directly from La Zisa, but then modified and adapted. At La Zisa there are in fact two pools fed by a source in the wall opposite the entrance via a marble canal in the floor. Here, the sound of running water was maintained by the installation of a fountain fed from a special water tank on the roof of the house. The pool was originally in white marble, replaced by Leighton when it cracked in the 1890s. The capitals of the columns at the entrance to the space do not

replicate those at La Zisa but instead feature two contrasting pairs of birds modelled by Randolph Caldecott. Caldecott (1846–86) gained international fame as an illustrator of children's literature in the 1880s but prior to this had taken classes in modelling from the French sculptor Jules Dalou, then living in Chelsea. A cast of one of his earliest bas-reliefs of a hunting scene and two drawings were purchased by George Aitchison, and it was through Aitchison that he received this commission. He was paid £10 10s in December 1880.

From the gold mosaic frieze upwards the Arab Hall diverges markedly from La Zisa, principally in the use of a dome instead of the complex geometry of La Zisa's *murqarnas*. Some reference is made to them in the four squinches that span the corners of the room, but these are hollow and functionless. According to Crane, Leighton's original intention was to let him and Burne-Jones loose on the dome but this never happened. Instead it was covered in gold leaf with stencilled decoration designed by Aitchison but again inspired by models

found in mosques in Turkey and elsewhere. The painted decoration was carried out by Harland & Fisher, ecclesiastical decorators of Southampton Street, who were paid £462 between June 1880 and the following February. The original decoration was painted over in the post-war period, but following extensive uncovering and analysis, it was recreated as part of the 2009–10 restoration. Set into the side of the dome are eight panels of coloured glass. These were obtained in Damascus by William Wright, the source for many of the tiles. Accounts then differ but it appears that all except one were destroyed in transit and replicas were made in England, 'a fact of which the owner is very proud'.

In the centre of the space hangs the brass gasolier converted to electricity in the 1890s. The form of the fitting, with a ring suspended from a single pendant, is typical of those found in mosques in the Middle East: Leighton made drawings of examples in Damascus in 1873. Around the circular base are birds with outstretched wings, made in brass to contrast with the copper ring. The fitting was made to Aitchison's design by Forrest & Son, manufacturers of oil and gas chandeliers of St Bride Street, Ludgate Circus. At the apex of the three pointed arches on each side of the room gas pipes can be seen emerging from the wall. It is possible that these originally fed further light fittings that illuminated the dome above, although no contemporary description refers to them. Forrest & Son were paid a total of £174, the final payment being

from the late sixteenth century.

Set into the wooden screen designed by Aitchison at the back of the recess on the west wall is a set of four 'Kubachi' tiles made in Persia in the early seventeenth century, remarkable for the fine painting of the human figure on each tile. Over the entrance is a spectacular panel of 42 tiles carrying verses from the Koran in a bold *muhaqqaq* script. The text is from the Surat Ar-Rahman, surah 54, verses 1–6 and reads:

> In the name of the merciful and
>   long-suffering God,
> The Merciful hath taught the Koran,
> He hath created man and taught
>   him speech.
> He hath set the sun and the moon in
>   a certain course,
> Both the grass and the trees are
>   subject to him.

The marbles used in the Arab Hall were supplied by White & Sons of Pimlico Road at a cost of £771. Considerable as this sum was, according to Aitchison, Leighton had been constrained to 'use the marbles that he could afford.' The large columns at the entrance to the room had to be the relatively inexpensive Caserta marble. They

made in April 1882.

Perhaps the most significant contributor to the success of the interior was the potter William De Morgan. His task was to make sense of the vast number of tiles that were now to be built into the room. Almost all are from Damascus and date from the sixteenth and early seventeenth centuries. Many had been damaged either as they were prized from their original locations or in transit to London. One account suggests that there were in fact insufficient tiles to complete the room, requiring De Morgan to 'fake' additions. However it is certain that De Morgan carried out repairs and where tiles were missing, made replicas. He then,

presumably with Leighton and Aitchison's close involvement, decided how the various borders and families of tiles would be most effectively displayed. For De Morgan, it was a unique opportunity both to work with an exceptional collection of original material and to master the processes and techniques involved in making replicas. Analysis of the glazes on the tiles carried out as part of the 2009–10 refurbishment indicates De Morgan was responsible for between 20 and 30 of them. Some are more evident than others. In the south-east corner of the room, a panel contains a pair of parrots perched on a fountain: on the left is De Morgan's, on the right the original dating

70 The decorative geometry of the Arab Hall dome revealed in a photograph taken from directly below.

71 The exterior of the Arab Hall from the north, illustrating the somewhat uncomfortable junction between it and the original house. The distinctive brick ziggurats set around the parapet had become unsafe and were removed in 1959. They were reinstated in 2008 using specially commissioned handmade bricks.

stand on bases of Belgian blue. The walls behind them are lined in Genoa green. Aitchison did not consider this combination a success: the blue and green were 'hardly to be distinguished in daylight', and 'very strong contrasts' were necessary if marbles in shade were to show sufficiently. Around the room is a dado in Irish black. The small columns in the angles of the walls in white marble do successfully stand out against niches in red Devonshire spar. Their bases are of Irish green. Irish green was also used for the string course above the gold mosaics, but when the block was cut it

disappointingly turned out to be a dull grey: perhaps on this occasion Leighton had to settle for second best.

The mosaic floor was designed by Aitchison and made by Burke & Co. of Newman Street, pioneers of the revival of mosaic production in Britain. Aitchison's designs in contrasting black and white marble are broadly Roman in inspiration, but the decorative patterns are not. In the Arab Hall, the interlinked flower motif around the border appears to derive from the mosaic decoration in the Dome of the Rock, Jerusalem. The floors in the adjacent

Narcissus Hall, using pink and grey marbles, and in the staircase hall beyond, with its more classically-inspired motifs, were designed to be read in the context of each space as well as establishing continuity across the whole of the ground floor.

The gold mosaic frieze was designed by the art-worker Walter Crane (1845–1915), a prolific and versatile painter, designer, writer, teacher and campaigner who remains best known as an illustrator of children's literature. Crane was initially approached by Aitchison to become involved in the decoration of the Arab Hall

and was paid a total of £338 between 1880 and 1883. The panels were made in Venice by Salviati & Co., a firm founded in 1859 to revive the ancient techniques of enamel and glass mosaic. The process involved firing a piece of gold leaf onto a ground of thick glass or enamel which was then fused onto more glass. The top piece of glass might be tinted for subtle gradations of colour and the ground could be produced in coloured enamels in place of gold leaf. To reduce costs and allow easy transportation of panels all over Europe, the firm developed a method of sticking tesserae onto brown paper using a water soluble glue. The completed panel was shipped and cemented into position, and once set, the brown paper was washed off the face. The firm rapidly became established: the Albert Memorial was one of its first commissions in England and was followed by many others.

Prior to starting work Crane recalled being sent a photograph of the original mosaics at La Zisa: in the recesses on the north and south walls, as requested, he repeated the same format of three roundels on a gold ground. The designs for each roundel were submitted to Leighton for approval and he retained some of them at the time of his death. Not all were equally pleasing to him: 'cleave to the Sphinx and the Eagle, they are <u>delightful</u>. I don't like the Duck-women'. The 'Duck-women' were Crane's interpretations of Sirens 'after the traditional treatment in Greek gems'. The eagle fighting with a snake is located centrally on the north wall, with sphinxes bearing flaming torches in the roundels on either side. The returns contain single roundels featuring the signs of the zodiac against a night sky, a response to Leighton's suggestion that they should contain 'the starry heavens'. On the south wall, a stylised Mediterranean round boat occupies the central roundel with mermaids substituted for the unsuccessful sirens. The returns contain the sun and moon rising over the sea. The roundels are interspersed with orange trees entwined by snakes, and at each end is a potted cypress tree with a mouse perched on the vessel.

The inclusion of animals and birds is a playful feature of the rest of the frieze, which appears to take elements from the mosaics at St Mark's, Venice. There are four panels of confronted peacocks in the corners of the room, while cockatoos perched amidst vines are on the east wall. In the east wall recess, two sets of confronted deer are set against foliage scrollwork in which sit squirrels, exotic birds and lizards. The roundels at La Zisa are interspersed with vines very similar in treatment to the mosaic decoration on the inner faces of the three arches – although these may have been designed by Aitchison rather than Crane.

The Arab Hall was not built for a practical purpose but as an atmospheric and memorable setting for Leighton's tiles. However no Arabian Nights fantasies followed within its walls. Instead, it was used simply as an after-dinner smoking room as Ernest Rhys recalls:

> After a dinner party at which Sir E. Burne-Jones, Mr Whistler, Mr Albert Moore and many others were present, I recollect how when we were smoking and drinking coffee in this hall, somebody, excitedly discoursing, stepped unaware right in to the fountain. Two large Japanese tench, whose somnolent existence was now for the first time made interesting, dashed about looking for an exit, and there was a general noise of splashing and laughter.

The Library

Leighton's library or study was added as part of the 1877–81 extension. As in the drawing room opposite, the fireplace is positioned directly beneath the window. Here Leighton attended to his substantial daily correspondence. By the late 1880s this had risen to such a level that a secretary was occasionally employed to assist with it. Here too Leighton dealt with Royal Academy affairs, although his biennial Presidential lectures were usually written in Perugia in Italy where he could work uninterrupted and then commit his subject to memory.

The bookcases around the room are original and contained much, though not all of Leighton's library: books were also piled on tables in the studio and shelved in the large bookcases designed by Aitchison that sat in front of the studio screen. The prominence with which they were displayed through the house served to underline Leighton's intellectual and scholarly inclinations. The walls were hung with many drawings and etchings including works by Jean-Auguste-Dominique Ingres, Alfred Stevens, Val Prinsep and Alphonse Legros. Together with other works known to have once been owned by Leighton, some of these have been reproduced as facsimiles and hung to conform to the one known photograph of this interior.

Leighton's writing desk was designed by George Aitchison as variant of a standard pedestal desk. The original was sold in 1896 and is untraced. A replica was commissioned as part of the 2009–10 restoration in order to once more communicate the purpose and function of this space. Behind the desk hangs *The Apotheosis of Marcantonio Bragadino*, attributed to the school of Tintoretto and painted in the late sixteenth century.

Until the 1980s this interior was still in use as a staff room. Restored first in the late 1980s, it was completely redecorated in 2009–10. Evidence for the colour came from an article published in July 1883 in *The Argus*, an Australian daily newspaper, which described the library as being painted a 'sober sage-green'. Armed with this information, the paint layers were sampled and a sage green was duly identified and matched. The curtains are *Tulip* designed by William Morris. A contemporary account of a visit to the house made by the art historian Julia Cartwright describes them hanging in place. Period photographs show the same fabric in use elsewhere in the house.

Antechamber & Silk Room

On the upper part of the staircase hung George Frederic Watts' portrait of Leighton of 1871 and close by was Leighton's own portrait of *Sir Richard Burton*, completed in 1876 and presented to the National Portrait Gallery after his death (pl.14). Sir Joshua Reynolds' unfinished double portrait,

76 *The library, showing* The Apotheosis of
Marcantonio Bragadino *above the bookcase and the
replica of Leighton's writing desk in the foreground.*

77 *The view from the Silk Room across to the two
doors into the studio.*

*Charles Watson, 2nd Marquess of Rockingham
with Edmund Burke* begun in 1766 (pl.31)
hung prominently above the blue tiles.
Prominence is also given to the copy of
Michelangelo's Creation of Adam from the
ceiling of the Sistine Chapel, Rome. Painted
by an unidentified French artist, the copy
intriguingly replicates the cracked and
marked surface of the original. The frame is
cemented into the wall and we can assume
that the staircase was designed in part to
accommodate the canvas, perhaps acquired
in Paris in the late 1850s.

At the top of the staircase when first
built was just a small landing connecting
Leighton's bedroom and the studio. This
remained a very public part of the house
and the door to the bedroom was deliberately tucked out of sight, buffered by its own
small lobby. With the 1877–81 extension, the
external wall was taken out and a new small
painting room or antechamber created over
the Narcissus Hall below. At the end of it
was installed the zenana believed to have
been acquired in Cairo, affording glimpses
into the Arab Hall and allowing the sound
of the fountain to trickle into the upper
floor of the house. The space is screened off
from the staircase by a curtain and large rug
supported on a timber frame. A new door
was knocked through, replacing what had
previously been a window, to provide separate access into the studio, and the room
seems to have functioned as a secondary,
more informal painting room, well lit by the
large domed roof-light. Leighton referred to
it as his 'den': here he could work or receive

78 *The antechamber, photographed in 1891.*
Tintoretto's Portrait of an Elderly Gentleman
can be seen hanging over the fireplace.

79 *The Silk Room.*

friends in a more intimate setting than the studio itself.

In front of the alcove stands Leighton's sculpture *Needless Alarms* and elsewhere were further examples of his Old Master collection, including a *Madonna and Child* attributed to Sano di Pietro da Siena, a *Head of a Man* attributed to Jacopo Bassano and *Jupiter and Semele* attributed to Andrea Schiavone. Above the fireplace on the south wall hung the *Portrait of an Elderly Gentleman* by Jacopo Tintoretto, acquired like several other works in Leighton's collection from the artist, dealer and collector Charles Fairfax Murray.

The construction of the winter studio in 1889–90 meant that the antechamber was no longer needed as a painting room and in 1894, the south wall was taken down and the Silk Room constructed beyond as the final addition to the house. The wall was replaced by two 'monolithic columns of pavonazzetto (marble) with bases and carved capitals of black Numidian'. Again lit by a large domed roof-light, the walls were lined with a 'warm faced leaf-green silk' which was run through into the antechamber, and hung with works by Leighton's friends and contemporaries. Pride of place was given to *Shelling Peas* by John Everett Millais, presented in 1889 by the artist in return for the cast of Leighton's *Needless Alarms* of 1886, admired by Millais and given to him. Here also were *A Corner of the Studio* presented by Lawrence Alma Tadema, and three canvases gifted by G.F. Watts, *Haystacks*, *Venus* and *Hope*. On the east side of the room a recess was created, lit by a small central roof-light and two light fittings set into the ceiling on either side. This appears to be the final example of the house being configured to display a particular object. In this case it was an important armorial tapestry bearing the arms of the English monarchs Willam III and Mary II, made between 1689 and 1695 by the Brussels weaver Hieronymus Le Clerc. The recess both protected it from direct sunlight and gave it an added status within the room.

The original silk lining of the room was removed in 1926 and the light fittings and other traces of the decorative scheme were lost in the years before or after the Second World War. In 1983, a section of the ceiling collapsed, initiating a complete restoration. A patterned woven damask was hung at this time. In 2010 a new silk was woven in Suffolk based on a sample of an 1880's silk found in a private collection; George Aitchison's watercolour of the interior and the only known period description of the colour as a 'warm faded leaf-green'. The accompanying braid was manufactured in Derby using the same dye produced for the silk itself.

80 *The vista from the studio through to the Silk Room.*

81 *The studio in spring 1895, with Leighton's final submission to the Royal Academy on display for the annual Show Sunday. On the far right is his celebrated Flaming June.*

The Studio

'Your mind travels back in imagination to the studio of one of the princely artists of Italy, to be brought back, however, to these modern days by a touch of nineteenth century colour or some latterday device of comfort', wrote Joseph Hatton of a visit to the studio in 1883. The life of the house revolved around Leighton's painting studio. Here he worked for several hours of almost every day that he was at home. Painting entirely alone, he deployed enormous effort and concentration in the creation of each painting. But the studio was not just a workshop, it also served as Leighton's principal reception room and the venue for his famous annual musical events.

The appearance of the unfurnished studio today is very different from the artistically cluttered space it was in Leighton's time. Then, his numerous easels were ranged across the front of the screen at the east end of the room, supporting works in different stages of completion. Other canvases were propped against furniture or on the many chairs around the room. The smells of oils, paints and varnish combined with those from the three fireplaces that originally warmed the room (a large fireplace located to the left of the main studio window is now blocked up). The considered informality of the interior was commented on by many in accounts of Leighton's house through the 1880s and 1890s: Hatton noted 'the rich rugs that lie here and there, excellent keys for colour, the tables crowded with books and sketches, the portfolios with studies of the figure,

nude and draped, the cozy fire at the other end of the room'. The south wall was lined with the oil sketches Leighton made on his many travels to Italy, Spain, Egypt, Turkey, Algeria, Greece, Syria and, nearer to home, Ireland and Scotland. Above them, running the length of the room, was a cast of the Parthenon frieze from the British Museum.

The sheer scale of the studio signalled its significance. When first built it was smaller than today, with the external wall at the east end standing on the line of the large screen. It nevertheless still measured 7.6m × 11.9m. In 1869, the studio was lengthened by some 4.5m. The gallery was dismantled and re-erected on the line of the original external wall in a modified form: it now served to hold up the ceiling at this end of the room. The service staircase was also substantially reordered so that the model emerged into the studio behind the new screen and

the former access to the left of the large fireplace was blocked up. Behind the screen, an area for the model to change and rest between poses was created, warmed by a small fireplace adjacent to the new model's entrance. Two stained glass windows in a 'Moorish' style, designed by Aitchison, were set into the east wall – the earliest example of oriental design to be installed in the house (pls 83, 97). One reason for the extension was to create a large under-floor store. Accessed via a trapdoor, it runs the full width of the studio and made a substantial space where canvases and studio clutter could be tidied away.

Practical considerations are evident elsewhere in the studio. Good but indirect natural light was essential. The studio was on the first floor for this reason, and the room is dominated by the large north-facing window. Beneath it stands the platform

82 *The studio looking west to the apse with its gilded semi-dome. At the right is the large north-facing window beneath which Leighton displayed a selection of drawings, plaster casts and maquettes. The black panel to the left of the stage at the far end of the room is the picture slot through which large canvases were taken in and out of the studio. The fireplace at the far right was recreated as part of the 2009–10 restoration.*

83 *One of Aitchison's designs for two stained glass windows in the studio extension, February 1870 (see pl.97).*

where the model might pose. A complex series of pulley blinds enabled Leighton to modify the light that fell across the model beneath.

The problem of how to get large canvases in and out of the studio was addressed by incorporating a tall, narrow door in the south-west corner of the room. This opened directly onto the exterior of the building allowing canvases to be passed through and winched down to ground level. The later construction of the Arab Hall made the picture slot unusable.

In addition to creating a private area for the model, the screen at the east end of the room had a number of other functions.

Behind it a purpose-made cabinet stored Leighton's colours and materials in 'endless compartments and pigeonholes'. A 'delicate winding staircase' gave access up onto the balcony. From here, Leighton could work on the upper reaches of a large canvas avoiding the hazards of balancing on a ladder.

The screen was also incorporated into Leighton's famed musical evenings. The Hungarian violinist Joseph Joachim was a regular participant and Leighton wrote enthusiastically to his sister following one performance in 1871:

> You heard no doubt that I gave a party the other day, and that it went off well. To me perhaps the most striking thing of the evening was Joachim's playing of the Bach Chaconne up in my gallery. I was at the other end of the room, and the effect from the distance of the dark figure in the uncertain light up there, and barely relieved from the gold background and dark recess, struck me as one of the most poetic and fascinating things that I remember. At the opposite end of the room in the apse was a blazing rhododendron tree, which looked glorious when it reached up into the golden semi-dome.

Leighton's original screen was taken down in 1935 to increase the seating capacity of the room.

The studio was restored in the mid 1980s, with a second substantial phase in 1997

when the room was completely redecorated, including the re-gilding of the half-dome at the west end and the quarter domes at the east end. In 1999, following an appeal by the Friends of Leighton House and as a memorial to Stephen Jones (1954–96), curator of Leighton House Museum from 1982 to 1989, the studio screen was re-erected on the basis of contemporary photographs and descriptions.

In 2009, the room was redecorated once more using a flat emulsion paint to replicate the dead finish of the distemper used by Leighton. The strip-flooring that had been introduced throughout the first floor in the 1960s or 70s was removed to reveal the original boards beneath. These had been stripped, but were otherwise intact and well preserved. They were re-stained to match areas where the original finish remained.

Between the two doors to the studio stands an inlaid cabinet (pl.25). An amalgamation of elements from earlier English and South German furniture it was made in the nineteenth century and stood in this position in Leighton's day. The piece returned to the house in 2011 from Australia where it had been bought at auction by a private collector in 1997.

The Bedroom

Leighton's bedroom, perhaps the only truly private room in the house, contrasts markedly with the rest of the interiors. Its modesty suggests a side to his character that rejected the grandeur evident elsewhere,

84 *Leighton's bedroom.*

85 *Leighton's bedroom as it appeared at the time of his death.*

86 *Chaucer's Dream of Good Women by Edward Burne-Jones, 1865.*

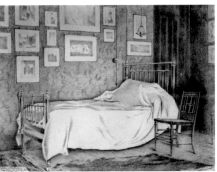

taking refuge in simpler surroundings. The skirting boards and door surrounds are unostentatious and conventional. Rather than a bespoke decorative finish as employed elsewhere, the walls were hung with a William Morris *India* wallpaper. Pictures were almost entirely limited to photographic reproductions of Old Master paintings admired by Leighton, an exception being Edward Burne-Jones' *Chaucer's Dream of Good Women* that hung opposite the fireplace. The room was sparsely furnished, containing Leighton's bed made by Winfield, a Dutch marquetry chest of drawers and some occasional chairs.

In the north-east corner a door led up three stairs to a toilet, and a second door in the opposite corner connected through to the adjacent bathroom/dressing room.

The original decorative scheme was reinstated in 1995–6 and the room furnished in 2000. The bed is identical to Leighton's though slightly narrower. The photographs were reproduced from the collection at Linley Sambourne House and framed in accordance with the detailed description of the room made after Leighton's death.

The Winter Studio

The winter painting studio constructed in 1889–90 provided additional painting space for use when daylight was poor and was screened from the studio itself by curtains. Here Leighton also stored his artist's props and materials, including a stuffed leopard, an assortment of shoes and sandal straps, costumes and lay figures. On the wall hung a large Persian carpet. The doors opening onto the balcony allowed air to circulate in the heat of the summer, and from the balcony there were views over the garden and across to the homes of his fellow artists and neighbours. In the winter, the room was heated by a stove and Leighton was evidently pleased to be able now to take advantage of the winter light. Writing to G.F. Watts in 1891 he noted 'today for instance the light in the glasshouse was lovely – limpid and mellow'.

The Garden

The garden was restored in 1997 with the support of the Heritage Lottery Fund, on the basis of a plan of the house and garden dating from 1896. This showed the formal beds immediately in front of the house, and a large expanse of lawn with herbaceous borders around the perimeter. A trellis covered part of the path running up the west side of the garden. Investigative work by

87 *Plan of the house and garden included in the auctioneer's brochure produced for the proposed sale of the house, 1896.*

88 *The house seen from the back of the garden, c.1896.*

89 *The house seen from the garden.*

English Heritage confirmed the position of these elements and determined that the two mounds on either side of the lawn had been landscaped when the garden was originally laid out. They were evidently planted with two substantial trees that more or less obscured the house when viewed from the back of the garden.

Although Leighton's friendship with Gertrude Jekyll may have led to some informal garden advice, there is no evidence of this and while visitors noted its scale and attractiveness, there is no sense of Leighton lavishing the same attention on the garden as on the house. Nevertheless, an account by Frederick Pepys Cockerell of summer Sunday mornings spent with Leighton is evocative:

> The quiet, the sun overhead, the grass under our feet, the green trees around us, and the house visible between them, form an ineffaceable picture of aesthetic contentment it is a delight to recall.

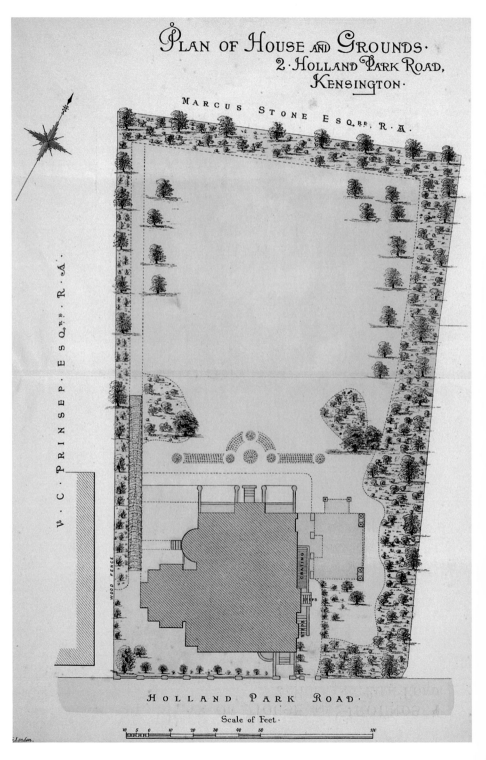

PLAN OF HOUSE AND GROUNDS.
2. HOLLAND PARK ROAD,
KENSINGTON.

MARCUS STONE ESQRE, R.A.

V. C. PRINSEP ESQRE, R.A.

WOOD FENCE

HOLLAND PARK ROAD.

Scale of Feet.

Life and Work at 2 Holland Park Road

90 *The dining room with the table set for one.*

91 *Leighton at work in the studio. At the rear to his right is one of the untraced pair of matching bookcases designed for the studio by George Aitchison.*

The whole year was planned out beforehand – the days on which he received visits, those of work; the hours in which he would see his few intimate friends, and those in which he would return their visits; even the day and hour for going to see his father.

GIOVANNI COSTA, 1897

As Leighton's reputation grew so did the demands on his time. The competing pressures of his work in the studio, the affairs of the Royal Academy, his large personal correspondence and his devotion to numerous causes, not least the Artists' Rifles of which he was Colonel until 1883, led to an almost fanatical discipline in the conduct of daily life. 'He made a mosaic of his days', wrote George Aitchison, 'in which every hour was set down, with its appointed task, and he allowed nothing to interfere with that part which related to his work.'

On a typical day at home, work in the studio might start at 8.30am, before which Leighton had breakfasted, opened his post, glanced at *The Times* and 'read for three quarters of an hour besides'. After a break for lunch between midday and 1pm, work continued until 5pm. After this he would attend to his correspondence before leaving to dine, usually alone at the Athenaeum, at 7pm. At twilight as he passed by, 'Mercutio' noted, 'you might catch sight of his figure sitting

motionless in his brougham alone'. Earlier in his career, Saturday mornings were kept free for himself and only close friends might call. Aitchison recalled using these opportunities to discuss progress on the design and construction of the house. On Sunday afternoons Leighton was formally 'at home' and might welcome visitors of many nationalities: he would 'converse with them all one after the other in their own tongues'. However, it is clear from numerous accounts that younger artists clasping letters of introduction were admitted at other times during

the week, when Leighton would break off from painting to show them around the house and offer advice and encouragement.

Work and the Studio

Leighton's method of working was rooted in drawing. At the time of his death, the studio contained over one thousand sheets of studies made over the course of his career, including the sketchbooks he filled as a boy. The majority of the drawings were made from life, and the comings and

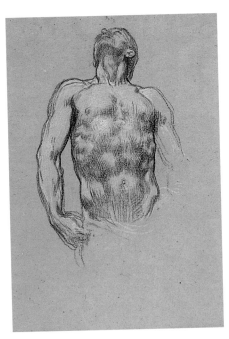

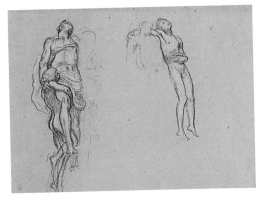

92 *Studies for 'And the sea gave up the dead which were in it'*, 1882–4.

93 *The oil sketch for 'And the sea gave up the dead which were in it'*, c.1891–2.

goings of models were frequent. According to Val Prinsep, Leighton was 'the last of the British painters who sought after the secrets of Titian', and in interviews he outlined a working method that was extraordinarily time-consuming and complex, and which purposefully echoed those of the Renaissance masters he so admired.

Once a composition had appeared in his mind's eye and had been fixed in an initial sketch, Leighton would seldom deviate from it. Instead, great energy and discipline went into drawing studies from the nude model conforming to his initial design. These would then be transferred to a single drawing of the whole composition that in turn would be enlarged and painted, in outline, onto the canvas. The nude figures were then shaded in monochrome to a high degree of finish. A small colour sketch was produced to fix the arrangement of colour across the composition, and further studies of draperies made in chalk on paper either from the model or the lay figure. Showing light,

shade and texture these would be enlarged without alteration and then painted in monochrome over the figures. Only once this underpainting was complete would the final stage, the application of colour, begin, taking much less time than the previous parts of the process. The highly technical and arcane subject of pigments, grounds, etc. – the chemistry of paints – fascinated Leighton. He once commented that he doubted whether any other artist enjoyed the process of *making* a picture as much as he did.

Several paintings might be in progress at once, with Leighton breaking off from one to work on another during the course of the day. Without the aid of a studio assistant, the completion of his major paintings was a process that from first conception through to exhibition could take months and on occasion years. The whole activity was centred on the studio on the first floor and structured around the submission to the Royal Academy's summer exhibition, which

opened in early May. Once the London season was over, Leighton and his fellow artists were free to travel.

Entertainment

From the start, Leighton had conceived the house as a venue for receiving guests and entertaining. The later extensions enhanced its capacity, forming a suite of interconnecting spaces on the ground floor that climaxed in the great talking point of the Arab Hall. As President of the Academy, Leighton welcomed many distinguished foreign artists to the house and made a point of entertaining all the forty Royal Academicians annually. Smaller groups or individuals were invited to dine on other occasions 'to meet other celebrities'. When not entertaining or invited out, Leighton would almost always dine at one of his clubs, but friends might be invited to breakfast with him. The artist J. McLure Hamilton recalled that the grilled bacon 'surpassed any I have ever seen or tasted'.

94 *A group of women viewing the Arab Hall,*
Graphic 2 June 1888, p.590.

95 *The violinist Joseph Joachim (1831–1907),*
one of the most regular participants in Leighton's
musical events.

Leighton's Sunday afternoon 'At Homes'
held between 3pm and 5pm were the most
regular occasions when the house was
on display and callers had the freedom
to explore the interiors and collections.
Through his involvement in the Kyrle
Society, founded to improve the lives of
the masses by fostering exposure to and
appreciation of beauty, Leighton allowed
access for visiting groups of 'the poor' under
the auspices of Octavia Hill. In his absence,
they could 'see everything but the studio',
he wrote. The South London Gallery was
a second philanthropic cause that took
up a great deal of Leighton's time. In 1878
pictures began to be shown in the library
adjacent to a Working Men's College and
exhibitions were subsequently organised in
Battersea and then Camberwell, where a
purpose-built gallery was erected. In 1887,
Leighton became Chairman of the Council
and regularly held meetings in the studio
with G.F. Watts and his wife Mary also in
attendance.

However it was on two occasions each
year that the house really came into its
own. The first was Show Sunday, usually
held at the end of March or early April on
the weekend before sending-in day for the
Royal Academy summer exhibition. Artists'
submissions for the year would be on show
in their studios, giving an invited public
– although many came without invitation –
the chance to see the major paintings of the
year ahead of the exhibition. At the same
time, the artist could gauge reactions and
might also make an advance sale. However,

the day was principally a social event, with
visitors coming as much to look through
the house and mingle with the artists as
to study their work. Vast crowds could be
expected, with hundreds passing through
over the course of the day. The houses of
the Holland Park Circle were a popular destination and Leighton's a particular draw.
Walter Crane, present in 1871, recalled 'the
courteous and princely way in which he
received his guests on these occasions, and
the crushes he had at his studio – Holland
Park Road blocked with carriages, and
all the great ones of the London world
flocking to see the artist's work'.

The second event that became a
fixture was Leighton's annual musical
recital. In Rome in his early twenties
Leighton had met and become entranced
by Mrs Adelaide Sartoris, one of the most
formidable opera singers of her day and
a member of the Kemble acting dynasty.
Music formed a central part of her frequent
'at homes'. Leighton had a good voice and

following lessons, willingly participated
as *primo tenore*. Later, when both were
established in London, he performed at her
musical gatherings, meeting and befriend-
ing many of Europe's foremost musicians.
But it was as the organiser of his own
annual 'musics', held in the spring every
year between 1867 and 1895, that Leighton
really expressed his passion. Friends would
be invited in the afternoon or early evening
for what was regarded as 'one of the real
treats of the year'. Performers included
the celebrated violinist Joseph Joachim
(pl.95), the pianists Charles Hallé and Clara
Schumann, and the cellist Alfredo Piatti.
Among the singers were two of the great
voices of the nineteenth century, Pauline
Viardot Garcia, and the baritone George
Henschel.

These evenings, combining the unique
setting of Leighton's studio with musical
excellence, left a profound impression on
those who attended. Edward Burne-Jones
and his wife Georgiana were always invited:

96 *The basement as it appeared in 1896, showing the layout of the service areas. Based on plans in* La Construction Moderne.

97 *Opposite: The pair of stained glass windows designed by George Aitchison set into the east wall of the studio extension in 1869–70 (see also pl.83).*

In March we went to the musical afternoon to which Leighton of his kindness bade his friends every year. There Joachim and Piatti used to be surrounded by lovers and friends, and to play in the way that artists do when every nerve is laid to rest by sympathy and every note is waited for and listened to. Who that was there can forget the feeling that ran through the room a second before the music began when Leighton took his seat to the left of the piano and uttered that tremendous 'Hush'!

Domestic arrangements

The domestic quarters at the house were, as was conventional, confined to the basement, with separate access on the east side of the building and an internal staircase linking all floors of the house. The Arab Hall extension was not accompanied by an equivalent increase in the size of the basement, which remained largely contained within the footprint of the original structure of 1865–6. However, the rearrangement of the reception area on the ground floor in 1877–81 was accompanied by the creation of a new servants' room below.

Accessed from an L-shaped corridor, the service areas were quite modest, reflecting the small number of domestic staff that Leighton retained. The cooking and food preparation areas consisted of a kitchen with cooking range (removed in 1952), a scullery, and a larder or cold store underneath the steps from the dining room to the garden. The wine cellar was next to the butler's pantry and bedroom. A strong room containing the household silver was located off the butler's pantry. The pantry and butler's bedroom were restored in 2009–10. Outside the basement door were a large underground coalbunker, built in 1877–81, and a storage area. The female staff slept at the top of house in two rooms above Leighton's bedroom. Although the spaces in the basement remain unaltered, virtually none of the original fittings survives and the rooms are used as the museum offices.

Up until 1881, just three staff – a butler, housekeeper/cook and housemaid – were employed with an additional tablemaid added by 1891. When he first moved into the house, Leighton employed a couple, Mr and Mrs Kendall, as butler and housekeeper. In 1872, Benjamin Kemp, two years his senior, became his butler and remained with him for twenty years. One visitor to the house, Julius Price, recalled that 'the door was opened by a manservant of impressive appearance – just the sort of servant one would have expected'. A succession of seven housekeepers came and went, of whom the last, Mrs Reid, was married to J. Sandercock (Sanders), who succeeded Kemp as butler up until Leighton's death.

It does not appear that Kemp or Sanders accompanied Leighton on his travels abroad and the housekeeper and housemaids were probably retained at home during these periods. With building or decorating works almost always going on in Leighton's absence, careful supervision from his staff would have been necessary. A major upheaval was the annual spring-clean of the studio that took place at the end of September each year.

Although Leighton appears always to have rented his horse and brougham, William Hogg was employed as his coachman from 1880. Leighton leased accommodation in the nearby Pembroke Mews off the Earls Court Road for Hogg, his wife and five children.

The Collections

Early Acquisitions, 1897–1927

The sale of Leighton's collections through Christie, Mason and Woods in the summer of 1896 allowed his sisters to settle bequests in accordance with his wishes, but left his house as an almost empty shell – a jewel box bereft of its jewels. The formation of a new collection was therefore a major preoccupation for Emilie Barrington and the Leighton House Committee; the body she helped establish to secure the building's long-term future as a museum (see p.31). Rather than attempting to re-form a version of Leighton's collections, the committee determined to commemorate his achievements by assembling a representative body of his own work to display through the interiors. The drawings and paintings they secured during this period remain the core of the museum's collections today.

At the time of his death, Leighton's studio contained some 1,600 drawings documenting his entire career. Shortly after his death these were sold by Leighton's sisters to the dealers, The Fine Art Society for £1000 and groups of drawings were then purchased by the British Museum, the Victoria and Albert Museum and the National Gallery of Ireland, as well as being sold individually to collectors. In December 1896, a deputation from the Leighton House Committee, including Leighton's neighbour, the sculptor Hamo Thornycroft, made a first selection of 180 drawings. Ultimately more than 1000 studies were acquired for the new museum, including gifts from the Prince of Wales, Thornycroft himself and G. F. Watts. Ironically, 500 were purchased for the museum by Leighton's sisters using the residue of the funds generated by the original sale of the drawings and the success of the Leighton sale at Christie's.

Drawings were not the committee's only interest. Appeals were made for gifts of relevant works and public subscriptions were sought to secure important paintings. Surprisingly few gifts were forthcoming from Leighton's friends and contemporaries. An exception was his near neighbour and long-time friend G. F. Watts who, no doubt with the encouragement of Emilie Barrington, presented two works which had been given to him by Leighton: *Study of a Male Figure* (cat.no.1) and his plaster maquette of *An Athlete Wrestling with a Python* (cat.no.26). The architect and Royal Academician Alfred Waterhouse, who had known Leighton since their meeting in Rome in the early 1850s, presented four drawings and three small paintings, all of which he had only recently acquired following the 1896 sale. The only other artist to present a work was the painter Briton Rivière, who donated a colour sketch for *Eastern Slinger Scaring Birds in the Harvest Time – Moonrise* (cat.no.6) of c.1875.

The most significant acquisition of the early years of the museum was purchased as a result of a public appeal, launched through *The Times* in 1909. The aim was to secure *The Death of Brunelleschi* (cat. no.29) from the son of Edward von Steinle, Leighton's inspirational master at the Städelsches Kunstinstitut in Frankfurt where he had trained. Painted in 1852

98   *Frederic Leighton, detail from* Orpheus and Eurydice, *c.1864 (cat.no.60).*

Mid-century additions, 1927–74

as Leighton's final work as a student, it was probably presented to Steinle before Leighton set off for Rome to embark on his professional career. Other significant purchases of this period were *Clytemnestra from the Battlements of Argos*, 1900 (cat.no.2), *Pavonia*, 1907 (cat.no.27), *Corinna of Tanagra*, 1908 (cat.no.28) and *A Noble Lady of Venice*, 1910 (cat.no.30). However, the acquisition of *The Death of Brunelleschi* had not been achieved without a struggle and no major works were bought by the committee after 1910; a reflection perhaps of the declining public interest in Leighton's work.

Small gifts continued to be made by those who had been close to Leighton. His younger sister, Augusta, died in 1919 bequeathing the landscape studies: *A Street in Damascus* and *Courtyard, Algiers* (cat.nos.31 and 32). In 1924 the artist John Hanson Walker, whom Leighton had used as a model in the 1860s (he sat for *Rustic Music*; cat.no.66) and encouraged to become a painter, presented Leighton's early portrait of his father, Frederic Septimus Leighton of 1849.

However, Emilie Barrington, who had been instrumental in setting up the museum immediately following Leighton's death and who assumed almost total responsibility for it as the new century progressed, emerges as the single most important donor of works. At least 17 pictures were presented by her, the majority making up the fine collection of Leighton's landscape sketches held at the museum.

Emilie Barrington's transfer of the house and almost all of its contents to the Royal Borough of Kensington in 1926–7 brought about a shift in the collecting policy of the museum. Where previously the focus had been almost entirely on Leighton, acquisitions were now made regardless of their relevance to him or even his contemporaries, as a broader and more contemporary municipal collection was formed.

The decline in Leighton's reputation reached its lowest ebb through the 1940s, '50s and '60s. This was a period when significant works by him might have been acquired at relatively little cost. However, only a single substantial Leighton purchase was made when *Orpheus and Eurydice* was bought in 1960 – itself an indication of how the focus of the museum had dissipated. Other paintings by Leighton, such as his portrait of the Hon. Frederick Wellesley, were gifts from the direct descendents of the sitter or presented by their first owner. In 1958, an intriguing collection of works were presented by the son of Leighton's last butler, John Sandercock and his wife, who was Leighton's housekeeper. The group of 21 items included drawings, watercolours and seven colour sketches in oil. A letter from Sandercock's son indicates that some, if not all of this material had been presented to his parents by Leighton, just before the artist's death. Others may have already been with the Sandercocks or were given to them later by Leighton's sisters in recognition of their service.

This period also saw the deaths of the last of Leighton's contemporaries, resulting in works by some of them entering the collection. Amongst them was his near neighbour, the sculptor Sir Hamo Thornycroft. Four years after he died in 1925, his widow Lady Agatha, presented a group of his wax maquettes, bronzes and the life-size *Lot's Wife*. Although not a neighbour, Alfred Gilbert, a second major sculptor of the nineteenth century, died in 1934 and two years later, following the dispersal of Gilbert's studio, a group of sketches and maquettes were presented to the museum by the National Art Collections Fund. Works by some of Leighton's other contemporaries, including Watts, Sandys, Dicksee, Millais and Byam Shaw, also came into the collection during this period, often from relatives of the artists concerned or with a provenance that linked them to members of Leighton's circle.

The modern era: 1975–2011

Leighton's relationship with his architect, George Aitchison, extended beyond their collaboration at Leighton's house. In the early 1880s, Leighton contributed two large friezes *The Dance* and *Music* (cat.nos.62 and 63) to the drawing room of 1 South Audley Street in Mayfair as part of Aitchison's scheme of decoration. These remained in situ until 1975 when both were presented to the museum prior to the sale of the property, an indication of a wider re-awakening of interest in Victorian art and design.

Throughout the 1980s the restoration of building, rather than the addition of works to the permanent collections, remained the priority for the museum. However, by the 1990s a series of focussed acquisitions were made that related to works already in the collections or extended the museum's holdings. In 1991, the colour sketch for *The Death of Brunelleschi* was reunited with the painting itself, acquired in 1909. In 1995 *Roman Mother* (cat.no.69), which had once belonged to George Aitchison was purchased; followed in 1996 by Leighton's portrait of his sister Alexandra, Mrs Sutherland Orr. From 2000 the rate of acquisitions accelerated, made possible by the combined generosity of the Friends of Leighton House Museum, the Heritage Lottery Fund, the Art Fund and the V&A/MLA Purchase Grant Fund. Works by Leighton remained the focus. His portrait of his great friend, the Italian artist Giovanni Costa was bought in 2004. A second portrait of a fellow artist, Charles Perugini followed in 2006. The acquisition of bronze casts of Leighton's *An Athlete Wrestling with a Python* (cat.no.72) and *Needless Alarms* (cat.no.74) in 2007 completed the museum's set of his small-scale sculpture.

Ironically, despite these additions, the museum still lacked a major late painting by Leighton. With many of the key works already in public collections and prices escalating, opportunities were scarce. So when the museum was offered Leighton's *Clytie* (cat.no.75), an unprecedented campaign

was launched to secure it. A powerful case could be built around the painting and what it could contribute to the commemoration of Leighton's life and achievements through the museum. The picture had remained unfinished in Leighton's studio at the time of his death. Exhibited at the Royal Academy as a memorial to him in 1896, the work is unusually revelatory, conveying a compelling sense of Leighton's despair at his failing health and the ending of his creative life. A fundraising campaign secured the money required and saw the return of the picture to the studio where Leighton had painted it and where it had been placed at the head of his coffin in January 1896.

The successful purchase of *Clytie* marked the end of one phase of acquisitions for the museum, as attention turned to the pictures and objects that Leighton had owned, rather than the works he had created. In 2004, the museum had acquired G.F. Watts' portrait of Leighton. An intimate and insightful image by his great friend and close neighbour, the portrait had belonged to Leighton and had hung prominently on the staircase of the house, giving it an added significance and resonance. This repatriation of items from Leighton's collection continued with the acquisition of Antonio Rossellino's *Madonna of the Candelabra* in 2005 for the Silk Room, where contemporary photographs showed it hanging to the left of Tintoretto's *Portrait of an Elderly Gentleman,* which itself had returned to the museum in 2001 following its acceptance by HM Government in lieu

of Inheritance Tax. The contribution that Leighton's collections could make to the atmosphere and authenticity of the interiors came into sharper focus with the refurbishment of the house and the redisplay of the contents in 2009–10. Other than within the studio, Leighton had very few of his own works on display in his house. To suggest the diversity of his interests as a collector, a number of works were loaned back to the house and hung in their original locations. Amongst them was a landscape by Giovanni Costa, *Brugnoletta in Noonday Repose,* which was subsequently acquired for the permanent collections in 2010. This new emphasis on re-introducing paintings, furnishings and objects that could reinforce the sense of the house as Leighton's home was given added impetus with the purchase of an inlaid cabinet once owned by him. The most important single piece of his furniture yet to return to the museum, it had emerged at auction in Australia in 1997 before returning in 2010 to the precise position in the studio from where it had been removed for sale in 1896.

Paintings and Sculpture by Leighton in the Leighton House Museum Collection

The following list includes all the oil paintings and sculpture by Leighton in the collection today. The museum's collection of Leighton's drawings was catalogued in 2006 with the support of the Heritage Lottery Fund and can be viewed on line at www.rbkc.gov.uk/leightonhousemuseum/drawings.

The works are presented in order of acquisition divided into three periods. Little documentation relating to the operation of the museum between 1897 and 1926 by the Leighton House Committee and its successor organisations, the Leighton House Society and the Leighton House Association survives. No precise date can therefore be established for when many items entered the collection prior to the transfer of the house to the Council in 1926–7. A series of early exhibitions were held at Leighton House from when it opened in 1900. The catalogues for these are held at the museum and provide a *terminus ante quem* for the acquisition of many of the works.

Measurements are framed, height × width. All works are oil on canvas unless otherwise stated.

An asterisk* indicates the work is illustrated here

99   *Frederic Leighton*, Clytie, 1895–6 (cat.no.75)

100   *Frederic Leighton*, Study of a Male Figure, *c*.1860 (cat.no.1)

1897–1926

1   *Study of a Male Figure, c.1860**
52.3 × 45.7cm
Provenance: Given by the artist to G. F. Watts; presented by him in 1897
LH 0382

2   *Clytemnestra from the Battlements of Argos Watches for the Beacon Fires which are to Announce the Return of Agamemnon, c.1874*
173.5 × 123.8cm
Provenance: Sir R. Pearce Edgecumbe; his sale, Christie's, 27–8 March 1896 (lot 271); Christie's, 6 June 1896 (lot 23), bought Goodall; acquired by 1900
LH 0372

3   *Entrance to a House, Capri, 1859*
45 × 38cm
Provenance: Artist's sale, 13 July 1896 (lot 211), bought Tregaskis; Emilie Barrington; presented by her by 1900
LH 0407

4   *Near Kynance Cove, Cornwall, 1890*
35 × 26cm
Provenance: Artists' sale, 13 July 1896 (lot 151); bought Wickham Flower; Emilie Barrington; presented by her by 1900
LH 0398

5   *Oil study related to one of the heads in 'Summer Moon', c.1872*
40 × 41.5cm

Provenance: Artist's sale, 11 July 1896 (lot 77), where it is described as a study for Clytemnestra; bought Thomas Agnew & Sons; Alfred Waterhouse RA; presented by him by 1900
LH 0383

6   *Colour sketch for 'Eastern Slinger Scaring Birds in the Harvest Time-Moonrise', c.1875*
25 × 22cm
Provenance: Fine Art Society; Briton Rivière RA; presented by him by 1900
LH 0405

101 *Frederic Leighton*, Palazzo Rezzonico, Venice, c.1880 (cat.no.13)

7 Oil Sketch of the landscape in 'David', c.1865

34 × 43cm

Provenance: Emilie Barrington; presented by her by 1900

LH 0411

8 Head of an Arab, 1868

41.5 × 31cm

Provenance: Artist's sale, 11 July 1896 (lot 36), bought Thomas Agnew & Sons, or lot 37, bought Charrington, or lot 38, bought Fine Art Society; Alfred Waterhouse RA; presented by him by 1900

LH 0396

9 Colour sketch for 'St George and the Dragon', c.1868

54 × 45cm (arched top)

Provenance: Emilie Barrington; presented by her by 1900

LH 0410

10 Head of an Old Italian Woman, undated

61.8 × 41.8cm

Provenance: Artist's sale, 11 July 1896 (lot 39), bought R. Wilson; Emilie Barrington; presented by her by 1900

LH 0380

11 A Pool on the Findhorn River, c.1890

20 × 25cm

Provenance: Artist's sale, 11 July 1896 (lot 74), bought Dickson or Dicksee, or lot 70, bought Thomas Agnew & Sons; Alfred Waterhouse RA; presented by him by 1900

LH 0416

12 Pasture, Egypt, 1868

21.5 × 45.5cm

Provenance: Artist's sale, 13 July 1896 (lot 226); bought Emilie Barrington; presented by her by 1900

LH 0403

13 Palazzo Rezzonico, Venice, c.1880*

37 × 31cm

Provenance: Artist's sale, 13 July 1896 (lot 177), bought Wickham Flower; presented by him by 1900

LH 0395

14 Martyrdom of St Justina after Veronese, c.1852

38 × 50.5cm

Provenance: Artist's sale; July 13 1896 (lot 247), bought Tregaskis; Emilie Barrington; presented by her by 1900

LH 0414

15 Head of an Italian Male, undated

80.5 × 67cm

Provenance: Artist's sale, 13 July 1896, part of lot 181, bought Emilie Barrington; presented by her by 1900

LH 0384

16 Head of an Italian Girl, c.1870

29 × 26cm

Provenance: Artist's sale, 13 July 1896 (lot 208), bought A. K. Hichins, or lot 213A, bought Leggato; Emilie Barrington; presented by her by 1900

LH 0417

17 Colour sketch for 'Boy with Shield Holding a Vase', c.1869

28 × 17.5cm

Provenance: Artist's sale, 13 July 1896 (possible lot 65), bought Leggato; acquired probably by 1900

LH 0404

18 A View in Spain, c.1866*

33 × 35cm

Provenance: Artist's sale, 11 July 1896 (lot 174), bought Emilie Barrington; presented by her by 1900

LH 0424

19 *Colour sketch for 'Idyll', c.1880–1**

22.5 × 32.5cm

Provenance: The Hon. Lady Leighton-Warren, presented by her by 1900

LH 0397

20 *Study of Hills, c.1879*

36 × 50cm

Provenance: Artist's sale, 13 July 1896 (lot 203), bought Emilie Barrington; presented by her by 1900

LH 0409

21 *A Coast Scene, Ireland: storm effect, 1874*

22 × 37cm

Provenance: Artist's sale, 13 July 1896 (lot 119), bought Drew, or lot 176, bought Potter, or lot 157, bought Thorpe; Emilie Barrington; presented by her by 1900

LH 0400

22 *On the Nile, 1868*

24.5 × 38cm

Provenance: Artist's sale, 13 July 1896 (lot 239), or 241 bought Dunthorne; acquired c.1903

LH 0422

102 *Frederic Leighton*, Damascus (Moonlight), 1873 (cat.no.23)

103 *Frederic Leighton*, A View in Spain, c.1866 (cat.no.18)

23 *Damascus (Moonlight), 1873*

40 × 28cm

Provenance: Artist's sale, 13 July 1896, lot 205, bought Sisley; Emilie Barrington; presented by her by 1903

LH 0423

24 *Pink Granite Boulders, Findhorn River, c.1890*

20 × 23cm

Provenance: Artist's sale, 13 July 1896 (lot 141); bought Emilie Barrington; presented by her by 1903

LH 0401

25 Taormina, c.1870–81

32 × 24cm

Provenance: Artist's sale, 11 July 1896 (lot 73), bought Charrington, or lot 75, bought John Hanson Walker; Countess of Lovelace, presented by her by 1903 · LH 0362

26 Maquette for 'An Athlete Wrestling with a Python', c.1874

24.5cm, plaster

Provenance: Given by the artist to G. F. Watts; presented by him by 1904

LH 0452

27 La Nanna (Pavonia), 1859

91.7 × 82cm

Provenance: Painted for George de Monbrison to replace the original which he gave up to the Prince of Wales; Christie's, 20 April 1907 (lot 109); purchased for Leighton House Museum

LH 0376

28 Corinna of Tanagra, c.1893

146.5 × 109cm

104 *Frederic Leighton*, The Death of Brunelleschi, 1852 (cat.no.29)

105 *Frederic Leighton*, Courtyard, Algiers, 1895 (cat.no.32)

Provenance: Stephen Holland; his sale, Christie's 25–9 June 1908 (lot 67), bought Sampson; purchased 1908

LH 0374

29 The Death of Brunelleschi, 1852*

287 × 227cm

Provenance: Professor Edward von Steinle; by descent to Dr Alphons von Steinle; purchased 1909

LH 0373

30 A Noble Lady of Venice, c.1865

116.5 × 95cm

Provenance: Sam Mendel; his sale, Christie's, 24 April 1875 (lot 423), bought Thomas Agnew & Sons; Lord Armstrong; his sale, Christie's, 24 June 1910 (lot 74), bought Mitchell; purchased 1910

LH 0375

31 A Street in Damascus, 1873

38 × 37cm

Provenance: The artist's sister, Mrs Augusta Matthews; bequeathed by her in 1919

LH 0421

32 Courtyard, Algiers, 1895*

34 × 25cm

Provenance: The artist's sister, Mrs Augusta Matthews; bequeathed by her in 1919

LH 0402

33 Dr Frederic Septimus Leighton, 1851

97 × 84.4cm

Provenance: John Hanson Walker; presented by him in 1924

LH 0371

34 A Boy Saving a Baby from the Clutches of an Eagle, 1850–2

49.5 × 50cm

Provenance: Acquired by 1926

LH 0364

35 A Garden Scene, c.1879–80

25.5 × 32.2cm

Provenance: Artist's sale, 11 July 1896 (lot 7); bought Emilie Barrington; presented by her by 1926

LH 0412

1927–1974

36 *An Italian Man, c.1864*

83 × 69cm

Provenance: Acquired by 1926

LH 0420

37 *On the Nile, 1878*

24 × 38cm

Provenance: Artist's sale, 13 July 1896 (lot 174), bought Emilie Barrington; presented by her by 1926

LH 0385

38 *A Persian Pedlar, 1852*

56.5 × 50.5cm

Provenance: B.G. Windus sale, Christie's, 14–17 February 1868 (lot 285), bought Cohen; N. Forbes Robertson; Christie's, 20 Feb. 1909 (lot 12); acquired by 1926

LH 0381

39 *Still Life of Fruit, c.1850*

41.5 × 49.5cm

Provenance: Acquired by 1926

LH 0049

40 *Study of Oak Leaves, c.1850–60*

42.7 × 43.8cm

Provenance: Emilie Barrington; presented by her by 1926

LH 0415

41 *Study of Rhododendron, c.1856*

54 × 43.8cm

Provenance: Emilie Barrington; presented by her by 1926

LH 0418

42 *A Sketch in Bedfordshire, c.1890*

38 × 42.5cm

Provenance: Artist's sale; 13 July 1896 (lot 161), bought Tregaskis; Emilie Barrington; presented by her by 1926

LH 0408

43 *Study of Landscape, Scotland, c.1890*

24.5 × 49cm; oil on board

Provenance: Probably artist's sale, 13 July 1896 (lot 191), bought Sisley; Emilie Barrington; presented by her by 1926

LH 0406

44 *Study of Landscape, Scotland, c.1890*

28 × 44.5cm; oil on board

Provenance: Probably artist's sale, 13 July 1896 (lot 191), bought Sisley; Emilie Barrington; presented by her by 1926

LH 0425

45 *View in Italy, with a cornfield, c.1860*

53.2 × 41.4cm

Provenance: Artist's sale, 13 July 1896 (lot 187); bought Wickham Flower; presented by Mrs Wickham Flower by 1926

LH 0386

46 *Woman Seated in a Landscape, c.1886–7*

41.5 × 31cm

Provenance: Artist's sale, 11 July 1896 (lot 72), bought Shepherd; presented by 1926

LH 0413

47 *Colour sketch for 'A Dream', c.1860–1*

36 × 25cm

Provenance: A. F. Shand; presented by him in 1932

LH 0390

48 *Elisha Raising the Son of the Shunamite, c.1881*

127 × 174cm

Provenance: Mrs Dyson Perrins; Mrs G.S. Potter; presented by her, 1937

LH 0377

49 *Vestal, c.1882–3**

91.5 × 73cm

Provenance: Miss Lucy Cohen; Lady Lucas, presented by her, 1945

LH 0378

107   *Frederic Leighton,* Colour sketch for 'Countess Brownlow', *c.1879*(cat.no.57)

108   *Frederic Leighton,* Orpheus and Eurydice: 'But give them me – the mouth, the eyes, the brows', *c.1864* (cat.no.60)

50   *Study for Desdemona, c.*1889

80 × 71cm

Provenance: Probably presented in 1947

LH 0393

51   *Mrs Williams, c.*1887

61 × 51.5cm

Provenance: Probably presented in 1947

LH 0387

52   *Bianca, c.*1881

70 × 56.5cm

Provenance: Arthur Lucas; Lady Lucas; presented by her, 1948

LH 0363

53   *The Hon. Frederick Wellesley,* 1851

155 × 106cm

Provenance: By descent to the sitter's son, Sir Victor Wellesley, presented by him, 1954

LH 0389

54   *Colour sketch for 'Electra at the Tomb of Agamemnon', c.*1869

19 × 16.5cm

Provenance: T.C. Sandercock; presented by him, 1958

LH 0366

55   *Colour sketch for 'Daedalus and Icarus', c.*1869

20 × 17cm

Provenance: T.C. Sandercock; presented by him, 1958

LH 0367

56   *Colour sketch for 'Antique Juggling Girl', c.*1873

13 × 9.5cm

Provenance: T.C. Sandercock; presented by him, 1958

LH 0370

57   *Colour sketch for 'Countess Brownlow', c.*1879*

35.5 × 28cm

Provenance: T.C. Sandercock; presented by him, 1958

LH 0365

58   *Colour sketch for 'Wedded', c.*1881–2

24 × 16.5cm

Provenance: T.C. Sandercock; presented by him, 1958

LH 0369

59   *Colour Sketch for 'And the sea gave up the dead which were in it',* 1891

20 × 20cm

Provenance: T.C. Sandercock; presented by him, 1958

LH 0368

60   *Orpheus and Eurydice: 'But give them me – the mouth, the eyes, the brows', c.*1864

168.3 × 151cm

Provenance: Alfred Brooks, sold by him, Christie's, 17 May 1879 (lot 103), bought Sully; Frances Reckitt; Terrence Rowe; Jerry Norman; purchased in 1960

LH 0392

61   *Mrs. Henry Evans Gordon (May Sartoris), c.*1875

121.5 × 127cm

Provenance: By family descent from the sitter to Lady Stanley of Alderley; sold by her, Christie's, 16 June 1961 (unsold), and again, 8 Dec. 1961, bought Douglas; Malcolm Young; presented by him in 1964

LH 0419

62 *The Dance, a frieze*, 1883

89 × 523cm

Provenance: Commissioned by James Stewart Hodgson for the drawing room at 1 South Audley Street, London; The trustees of the late Sir J.R. Ellerman, Bart.; presented by Lady Ellerman in 1975

LH 1049

63 *Music, a frieze*, 1885

85 × 523cm

Provenance: Commissioned by James Stewart Hodgson for the drawing room at 1 South Audley Street, London; The trustees of the late Sir J.R. Ellerman, Bart.; presented by Lady Ellerman in 1975

LH 1050

64 *Colour sketch for 'The Triumph of Music'*, *c.*1855–6

31 × 42cm

Provenance: James Knowles; his sale, Christie's 29 May 1908 (lot 32), bought Sampson; acquired by Leighton House Museum *c.*1980

LH 1823

65 *The Sluggard*, 1885*

53cm, bronze

Provenance: Christopher Wood Gallery; purchased with the assistance of the V&A Purchase Grant Fund, 1983

LH 0249

66 *Rustic Music*, 1861

91 × 91cm

Provenance: Fine Art Society, 1984; purchased with the help of the V&A Purchase Grant Fund and The Art Fund, 1984

LH 1102

109 *Frederic Leighton, The Sluggard, 1885*
(cat.no.65)

67 *Colour sketch for 'The Death of Brunelleschi', c.1852*

52.5 × 47cm

Provenance: Given by the artist's sister Mrs Augusta Matthews to Mr and Mrs John Hanson Walker; thence by descent; Christie's 14 June 1991, purchased with the assistance of the v&a Purchase Grant Fund, 1991

LH 1141

68 *Colour Sketch for 'Hercules Wrestling with Death for the Body of Alcestis', c.1869–71*

43 × 50cm

Provenance: Ernest & Phillips, London; Christie's, 5 March 1993 (lot 94), purchased with the assistance of the The Art Fund and the v&a Purchase Grant Fund, 1993

LH 2104

69 *Roman Mother, c.1867*

82.9 × 69.6cm

Provenance: George Aitchison PRIBA; his sale Christie's, 20 Feb. 1911 (lot 137), bought Smith; Sotheby's 6 November 1995 (lot 213), purchased with the assistance of the Friends of Leighton House Museum and 18 Stafford Terrace, 1995

LH 2165

70 *Mrs Sutherland Orr, 1891*

88 × 75.5cm

Provenance: By descent to Mrs M. Gadsby; Christie's 7 June 1996, purchased with the assistance of The Art Fund and the Friends of Leighton House Museum and 18 Stafford Terrace, 1997

LH 1765

110 *Frederic Leighton, Giovanni Costa, 1878*
(cat.no.71)

71 *Giovanni Costa, 1878**

73.5 × 64cm

Provenance: The sitter; thence by descent;
Christie's, June 1997 (lot 39); Private Collection;
Nevill Keating Pictures Ltd 2004, purchased with
the assistance of MLA/V&A Purchase Grant Fund,
The Art Fund and the Friends of Leighton House
Museum and 18 Stafford Terrace, 2004

LH 2187

72 *An Athlete Wrestling with a Python,* (*this cast c.1910*)

52cm, bronze

Provenance: Batchelor; Van de Klugt; thence
by descent to Anna Spencer; purchased with
the assistance of The Art Fund, the MLA/V&A
Purchase Grant Fund and private donations,
2005

LH 1212

73 *Carlo Perugini, 1855**

59.6 × 55cm

Provenance: The sitter, thence by descent;
Bonham's, November 2006 (lot 211), purchased
with the assistance of The Art Fund, the MLA
/V&A Purchase Grant Fund and the Friends of
Leighton House Museum and 18 Stafford Terrace,
2006

LH 3031

74 *Needless Alarms, c.1886*

51cm, bronze

Provenance: Private collection, England; the
Robert Bowman Gallery, London, purchased
with the assistance of The Art Fund and the
MLA/V&A Purchase Grant Fund, 2007

LH 3014

111 *Frederic Leighton*, Carlo Perugini, *1855*
(cat.no.73)

75 *Clytie, 1895–6**

156 × 136cm

Provenance: Fine Art Society, London;
Collection of Sir James Knowles, his sale,
Christie's, London, on 29 May 1908 (391);
Sampson; Ranjitsinhiji, then by family
descent; Private Collection; Sotheby's, London,
6 November 1995 (237); Private Collection;
Sotheby's, London, 4 June 1997 (154); Private
Collection: Nevill Keating Pictures Ltd,
purchased with the assistance of the Heritage
Lottery Fund, The Art Fund, the Friends of
Leighton House and 18 Stafford Terrace and by
public donations, 2008

LH 3015

76 *Colour Sketch for 'Cimabue's Celebrated
Madonna is Carried in Procession through the
Streets of Florence', 1854**

29.8 × 65.2cm

Provenance: B.G. Windus Esq; G.P. Wall,
Sheffield; Christie's, 16 March 1912 (lot 26); with
Cross & Phillips, Liverpool; W.H. Lever, 1st
Viscount Leverhulme; Lady Lever Art Gallery,
Port Sunlight, Wirral, Merseyside; Lady Lever
Art Gallery sale, Christie's London, 6 June 1958
(lot 135); with Gooden & Fox, London; John
Bryson, Oxford. His sale, Christie's, 13 May 1977
(lot 171); Mrs Tanenbaum by 1977; Sotheby's,
New York, 24 October 1996 (lot 113); private
collection; Christie's New York, 13 October 2011
(lot 57); purchased by Nevill Keating Pictures
Ltd on behalf of Leighton House Museum, with
the assistance of the Art Fund and the Friends of
Leighton House Museum and 18 Stafford Terrace

112 *Frederic Leighton*, Colour Sketch for 'Cimabue's Celebrated Madonna is Carried in Procession through the Streets of Florence', 1854 (cat.no.76)

Bibliography

Primary Sources

COUTTS BANK, LONDON: Leighton's account with Coutts is held as part of the bank's archives.

LONDON METROPOLITAN ARCHIVE: Uncatalogued papers relating to the Holland Estate together with papers relating to the proposed sale of the house to the London County Council in 1911 and the construction of the Perrin Gallery extension.

THE ROYAL ACADEMY LIBRARY: Leighton's notebooks and sketchbooks (LEI/1-LEI/41)

THE RIBA DRAWINGS COLLECTION: Aitchison's designs for Leighton House together with his beautifully rendered drawings for other interior commissions.

CHRISTIE MANSON & WOODS LTD, LONDON: The annotated catalogue for the sale of Leighton's collections in 1896 is in the Christie's archives.

HITCHMOUGH, Wendy: *Leighton House, Historical Documentation*, a survey commissioned by the Royal Borough of Kensington & Chelsea, February 1997 (one copy held at Leighton House Museum)

PUBLIC RECORD OFFICE: Papers relating to the valuation of Leighton's Estate etc (IR 59/168)

Leighton's Life and Work

AITCHISON, George: 'Lord Leighton, P.R.A.: Some Reminiscences', *Journal of Royal Institute of British Architects*, 3, 3rd series, 1896, pp.264–5

BARRINGER, Tim and PRETTEJOHN, Elizabeth, eds: *Frederic Leighton, Antiquity, Renaissance, Modernity*, New Haven & London, 1999

BARRINGTON, Emilie: *The Life, Letters and Work of Frederic Leighton*, 2 vols, London, 1906

BRANDLHUBER, Margot Th. and BUHRS, Michael, eds.: *Frederic, Lord Leighton, Painter and Sculptor of the Victorian Age*, exhibition catalogue, Prestel, 2009

CORKRAN, Alice: *Frederic Leighton*, London, 1904

COSTA, Giovanni: 'Notes on Lord Leighton', *Cornhill Magazine*, 2, March 1897, pp.373–84

DAKERS, Caroline: 'Leighton: The Truth? Frederic, Lord Leighton, and his Relationship with Lily and Fred Mason', *Apollo*, December 1996

GERE, Charlotte et al: *A Victorian Master: Drawings by Frederic, Lord Leighton*, exhibition catalogue, The Royal Borough of Kensington and Chelsea, 2006

JONES, Stephen et al: *Frederic Leighton*, exhibition catalogue, Royal Academy of Arts, London, 1996

HAMILTON, J. McLure: *Men I Have Painted*, London, 1921

HAWTHORNE, Julian: *Shapes That Pass: Memories of Old Days*, London, 1928

HOSMER, Harriet: *Letters and Memories*, ed. Cornelia Carr, London, 1913

'MERCUTIO': 'Observations', *The St James's Budget*, no.814, 31 January 1896

NEWALL, Christopher: *The Art of Lord Leighton*, Oxford, 1990

ORMOND, Leonée and Richard: *Lord Leighton*, New Haven & London, 1975

OWEN-JONES, Huw: *Ten Years in Damascus*, Matador, 2010

PENROSE, F.C.: 'Royal Institute of British Architects, The Royal Gold Medallist', *The Builder*, 30 June, 1894, p.495

PRINSEP, Valentine: *Lectures Delivered to the Students of the Royal Academy of Arts*, London, 1902

RHYS, Ernest: *Frederic Lord Leighton: An Illustrated Record of His Life and Work*, London, 1904

SIMON, Robin, ed.: 'Lord Leighton, 1830–1896, and Leighton House: a Centenary Celebration', *Apollo*, 143, February 1996

STALEY, Edgcumbe: *Lord Leighton of Stretton, PRA*, London, 1906

WRIGHT, William: 'Lord Leighton at Damascus and After', *Bookman* vol.9, March 1896, pp.183–5

Contemporary Accounts of the House and Contents

A.G.T.: 'The late Lord Leighton's bedroom, showing the bed on which he died', *The Art Journal*, 1896, pp.364–5

'An H. and C.R.I.B.A': 'Lord Leighton et son habitation de Holland-Park Road', *La Construction Moderne*, 14 March 1896, pp.217–20, 236–8, 242–4, 278–80

ADAMS, Maurice: 'Sir Frederick Leighton's House and Studio', *Building News*, 39, 10 October 1880, p.384

ANONYMOUS: 'House and Studio of F. Leighton, Esq., A.R.A., Kensington', *Building News*, 13, 9 November 1866, p.747

ANONYMOUS: *Building News*, 31, 22 December 1876

ANONYMOUS: 'Sir Frederick Leighton At Home, a chat with the President of the Royal Academy', *Pall Mall Budget*, 3 July 1890, pp.848–9

ANONYMOUS: 'Picture Gallery, 2 Holland Park Road', *Builder*, 69, 9 November 1895, p.336

BARRINGTON, Emilie: 'Lord Leighton's House and What It Contains', *Magazine of Art*, 22, October 1896, pp.529–34

BURNE-JONES, Georgiana: *Memorials of Edward Burne-Jones*, London, 1909

BUTLER, Virginia: 'An Hour at Sir Frederick Leighton's', *Lippincott's Monthly Magazine*, 52, 1893, pp.463–6

HATTON, Joseph: 'Some Glimpses of Artistic London', *Harper's New Monthly Magazine*, November 1883, p.828

HAWEIS, Mary: *Beautiful Houses: Being a Description of Certain Well-Known Artistic Houses*, London, 1882

HOW, Harry: 'Sir Frederick Leighton, P.R.A.', *Strand Magazine*, 4, 1892, pp.126–37

LANG, Leonora: *Sir Frederick Leighton: His Life and Work*, London, 1884

MCALLISTER, Isabel: *Alfred Gilbert*, London, 1929

PRICE, Julius: *My Bohemian Days in London*, London, 1914

Artists and Designers Involved in the Construction of the House

AITCHISON, George: 'The Learning of Architecture', RIBA *Journal* 9, February 1902, pp.193–200

AITCHISON, George: 'Marble', RIBA *Journal* 10, 1902–3, pp.529–37

BLACKBURN, Henry: *Randolph Caldecott, a Personal Memoir of his Early Art Career*, London, 1886

BURKE, William Henry: *A Short History of marble mosaic pavements and of the events connected with their modern revival*, promotional pamphlet, *c.*1900

CATLEUGH, John: *William De Morgan Tiles*, London, 1983

CRANE, Walter: *The Work of Walter Crane*, London, 1898

CRANE, Walter: *An Artist's Reminiscences*, London, 1907

DAKERS, Caroline and ROBBINS, Daniel: *George Aitchison, Leighton's Architect Revealed*, exhibition catalogue, The Royal Borough of Kensington and Chelsea, 2011

LAMONT, L.M.: *Thomas Armstrong, C.B. A Memoir, 1832–1911*, London, 1912

PORTER, Venetia: 'William De Morgan and the Islamic Tiles of Leighton House', *Journal of the Decorative Arts Society*, 16, 1992

RICHARDSON, Margaret: *George Aitchison: Lord Leighton's Architect*, RIBA Heinz Gallery, London, 1980

SALVIATI, Antonio: *On Mosaics (generally) and the superior advantages, adaptability, and general use in the past and present age, in architectural and other decorations of enamel mosaics*, London, 1865

Leighton House and the Holland Park Circle

BRYANT, Barbara: *G.F. Watts in Kensington: Little Holland House and Gallery*, Watts Gallery, 2009

CAMPBELL, Louise: 'The design of Leighton House, The artist's "Palace of Art"', *Apollo* 143, February 1996, pp.10–16

CAMPBELL, Louise: 'Decoration, Display, Disguise: Leighton House Reconsidered', in Tim Barringer and Elizabeth Prettejohn, eds, *Frederic Leighton, Antiquity, Renaissance, Modernity*, New Haven & London, 1999

DAKERS, Caroline: *The Holland Park Circle, Artists and Victorian Society*, New Haven & London, 1999

DAKERS, Caroline: *Artists At Home, The Holland Park Circle, 1850–1900*, exhibition catalogue, Leighton House Museum, 1999

FINDLATER, Julia: '100 years of Leighton House', *Apollo* 143, February 1996, pp.4–10

GERE, Charlotte: *Artistic Circles: Design*

Acknowledgements

Illustration Acknowledgements

and Decoration in the Aesthetic Movement, V&A Publishing, 2010

GOULD, Veronica Franklin: G. F. Watts, The Last Great Victorian, New Haven & London, 2004

HACKFORD, T. Reece: Lord Leighton's Arab Hall, MA diss. Brown University, 1981

LAMB, Joseph Frank: Lions in their Dens: Lord Leighton and Late Victorian Studio Life, phD/ umi dissertation, University of California, Santa Barbara, 1987

ROBBINS, Daniel, ed.: Closer to Home, The Restoration of Leighton House and Catalogue of the Reopening Displays, The Royal Borough of Kensington and Chelsea, 2010

SHEPPARD, F.H.W., gen. ed.: The Survey of London, Northern Kensington, 37, London, 1973

STELL, C.F.: 'Leighton House, Kensington', Archaeological Journal, 144, 1959, pp.122–5

The author would like to thank the enormously dedicated staff of Leighton House Museum for their contributions to the museum and this publication; Noé Auvélius, Sally Dobinson, Heather Fleming, Alex Fugger, Caroline Hill, Alan Kirwan, Steve Maney, Evelyn Francourt and Debbie Shipton.

Grateful thanks to the following for their advice and expertise:

Angela Bolger, John Burbidge, Louis Campbell, Caroline Dakers, Jane Davies, Graham Dobson, Charlotte Gere, Amin Jaffer, Ebeltje Hartkamp, Deborah Howard, Isabel Hernandez, Pamela Hunter, Rebecca Jallot, Hilde Johnson, Sue Kerry, Perilla Kinchin, Martin Levy, John Martin, Rheagan Martin, Angela Nevill, Shirley Nicholson, Richard and Leonée Ormond, Christine Powell, the Robbins family, Carrie Starren, Dante Vanoli, Dave Walker.

Special thanks to Philippa Martin for all her unfailing help and support.